The Way To Lasting Success

Unleash Your Limitless Potential, Elevate Goal Setting, Improve Thinking and Decision Making, and Create the Life You Want

SOM BATHLA

www.sombathla.com

Your Free Gift Bundle

As a token of my thanks for taking time out to read my book, I would like to offer you a gift bundle:

Click and Download your Free Gift Bundle Below

You can also download your gift at http://sombathla.com/freegiftbundle

More Books by Som Bathla

[The Science of High Performance](#)

[The Mindful Mind](#)

[Conquer Your Fear Of Failure](#)

[The Mindset Makeover](#)

[Living Beyond Self Doubt](#)

[Focus Mastery](#)

[Just Get It Done](#)

You may also visit my all books together at http://sombathla.com/amazon

Contents

Your Free Gift Bundle 2

More Books by Som Bathla...........................3

Part I: Introduction 6

    A Success Story That Didn't End Successfully.... 6

    What is Your Definition of Success? 19

    Set Quality Goals for LASTING Success 23

PART II: "You" Are the Starting Point of Your Success Journey...43

    Embrace Your Identity..................................... 43

    Are You Obsessed or Just Passionate? 51

PART III: Your Four Activity Zones and How to Reach Your Top Zone....................................61

PART IV: Harness the Power of Three 'S's in SUCCESS & Optimize Your Performance 79

PART V: Effective Ways to Level-Up Your Mental Game & Accelerate Your Success 92

    1.   Develop High Leverage Thinking 94

    2.   Determine Your Performance Necessity 107

    3.   Reprogram Your Mind by RWID Framework 113

4. Clarity Seeking Is Never Ending & How to Clear Your Thinking 123

5. Catapult Your Self-Image through Mental Training 133

6. How to Use Visualization To Design Your Future 141

7. Don't Rely on Willpower Solely 157

8. Ego Is the Enemy: How to Overcome It and Progress Faster 164

9. Redefine Failure: Fail Fast Forward To Success 172

Final Words 178

Thank You! 181

Part I: Introduction

******

"Success without fulfillment is the ultimate Failure." ~ **Tony Robbins**

A Success Story That Didn't End Successfully

People in the United States and most of the world loved this person. He started his career as a stand-up comedian in San Francisco and Los Angeles in the mid-1970s and established himself as a success icon through his leading show, *San Francisco's Comedy Renaissance.* He rose to the pinnacle of his fame through his comedy show *Mork and Mindy.*

For those few who don't know, I am talking about Robin Williams, the comedy star. But he didn't simply stop at comedy. He also gave himself the challenge to win an academy award by acting in films. He won 1997 Academy Award and besides that, in his entire career, he won two Emmy Awards, seven Golden Globe Awards, four Grammy Awards, to list a few[1]. By all measures. this man can be seen as a man of accomplishment, wherever he put his hands, he came out as a successful man– be it television or films, he left his own mark in the industry.

He was a master of the science of achievement by all means. But, surprisingly, he ended his life by hanging himself in his home in 2014, which shook the whole nation. I was watching Tony Robbins in one video[2] wherein he said that in all his events across the world, be it Australia, Beijing, Tokyo, United States, or Brazil, upon being asked whether people

---

[1] https://en.wikipedia.org/wiki/Robin_Williams
[2] https://www.inc.com/video/tony-robbins-why-success-without-fulfilllment-is-the-ultimate-failure.html

loved Robin Williams, 98-99% people raised their hands. He had tens of millions of fans in the world who cherished the joy spread by Robin Williams. Then Tony made one touching statement, "This man (Williams) made the whole world laugh with joy, except himself."

Despite having all the worldly pleasures and huge success in life, Williams ended up in depression took his own life. He was undoubtedly very successful, but the way he ended his life seemingly indicates that his success couldn't give his life meaning or fulfillment. Therefore, Tony Robbins rightly stated that *"Success without fulfillment is the ultimate failure."*

Different views have been expressed by people around the world, some stating that his suicide was due to his severe depression and associated mental illness. On the other hand, people like Tony Robbins, while praising Williams for being a good man, unquestionably adored by the whole world, stated that Williams had to end his life because he couldn't find fulfillment in his success to finally lead a happy life.

Without getting much into any controversy about the reasons for his ending his life, the message that one can draw out of the above life story is that merely material success in the world does not guarantee fulfillment or meaning in one's life.

The above life story of a legend is tragic on the one hand but more of a cautionary tale for people looking for achieving success in their lives, while disregarding the factors leading to true fulfillment.

We might think about ourselves that we'd be a holistic success once we reach a certain level or rank or achieve a specific income or wealth. We might think of ourselves as different and wonder why don't people feel happy after such huge achievements. We think there must be a problem with other people that would have led them to not feeling fulfilled or happy, but we think we would be truly happy once we achieve our goals in the world.

But, why do we think like this?

It is so because until we experience something personally, we don't believe other people's stories. For example, we daily hear the accidents happening around us. Every day the news tells us about the accidents, murders, or terrorist attacks happening somewhere around us and people dying. But think for a moment about how seriously you take these instances. At the maximum, you might feel sad for such accidents for a moment, but very soon you move on to the next news or next TV channel and forget the tragedies that happened to other people. However, if a similar accident or any other tragedy happens in our neighbour or God forbid in our own family, then the reactions are entirely on a different extreme. You may try to recall some death or any other mishap in the past in your family and you would remember that you had spent days, weeks, months, or sometimes years in deep sorrow missing your loved ones. This is so, because of human nature, we cannot truly understand the significance of certain things in our lives until we personally experience them through our blood and tears.

For this reason, when we hear the successful stories like the above that end so sadly, we often think ourselves to be different and can imagine that we may ever end up in such situation after achieving the material success or accomplishing our dreams. We continue to think that if we reach a particular figure, say *a hundred thousand dollars* or *a million dollars* or *multi-million dollars*, whatever our goal is, we'd be happy after that achievement. Of course, we would feel a temporary sense of achievement, but if your goals are not based on something which fulfills you, this sense of achievement will have a short life and soon you will find yourself looking for something else.

Why material success gives short-term happiness?

Whatever material things you achieve in the world, it gives happiness for only a short time, and soon it stops giving you any further pleasure. Why is it so? In fact, there is a research and study on human psychology known as a ***hedonic treadmill*** or ***hedonic adaptation***[3], which explains an observed tendency of humans to quickly return to a relatively stable level of happiness despite major positive events or life changes. According to this theory, as a person makes more money, expectations and desires rise in tandem, which results in no permanent gain in happiness.

---

[3] https://en.wikipedia.org/wiki/Hedonic_treadmill

Raj Raghunathan, author of the book, *If You're So Smart, Why Aren't You Happy?: How to turn career success into life success*, states certain necessary pre-requisites or needs for leading a successful as well happy life as below:

a. **Fulfillment of Basic Needs**: The first requirement of a human being is to provide for his food, clothing, and shelter – if one is not able to fulfill these needs, that are called "basic needs" then he cannot ever be happy. Since we are talking about successful people here, the first assumption is that the person has already met his basic needs. Therefore, beyond the basic needs, there are a few other important needs as stated below that are responsible for the happiness of successful people.

b. **The Need for Connection**: Then next need comes is the need for connection. Raghunathan states that as per one study that examined 10% of the happiest people of the world, it was found that they have at least one intimate relationship. Therefore, it was stated that sense of belongingness or intimate connection is not a luxury; rather, it is a necessity to be a part of the happiest group.

c. **The Need for Mastery**: The next human requirement is his need to be efficacious in whatever he or she chooses as a career. This need is for attaining mastery in one's chosen field of activity. We need to feel we are good at something, i.e., our profession, or hobbies, etc. If you don't feel you are good at something, then you won't be truly happy, and chances are you won't be able to earn big money.

d. **The Need for a Sense of Autonomy**: The last need is the need for being not controlled by anyone and being able to make decisions independently. That's the reason we want to resist situations where we don't have the freedom to do whatever we wish. Therefore, the desire for autonomy is wired into our brains like the desire for connection and mastery.

Further, Sonja Lyubomirsky, the author of the book, *The How of Happiness: A Scientific Approach to Getting the Life You Want,* suggests that "life circumstances" (such as education levels, marital status, wealth, etc.) contribute only about 10% to one's happiness, with the rest coming from one's genetic make-up (about 50%) and one's values, attitudes, and habits (about 40%).

The foregoing story and the studies give a strong message that one should not be choosing his goals and think he'd be successful merely upon achieving only the extrinsic or outside factors (more on that later) and rather consider his internal needs for happiness and fulfillment before investing one's life to achieve the chose dreams.

That's the reason the first section of the book is focused on success that should give you fulfillment and joy. Nobody wants to aspire to a success and then feel like a loser once he obtains it. If the goal you intend to pursue lacks the right underlying reasons, you will end up sacrificing the other important areas of life merely in the pursuit of your unhealthy goals. You will steal your family time or maybe compromise on your own health by putting longer hours on that goal. Also, you may end up missing your kids' moments of innocent childhood that you will not be able to enjoy later, after they grow up and move further in their own lives.

You know it well that whenever you say yes to anything in life, you say no to a lot of other things. After all, our lives are nothing but a sum total of time granted to us – and also very limited in time. Therefore, it is imperative that we be cautious in choosing where we spend our time and energy while choosing our goals.

This book is also about equipping you with necessary mental tools and strategies to fasten the pace of progress. But before you pace up and run with your toolbox, you need to make sure that the direction you are choosing is in alignment with your true north. You wouldn't prefer accelerating your vehicle and wasting your fuel or energy in driving faster on the wrong road, because it will take substantial time to come back and you would have already wasted your precious resources on something you didn't truly want.

You don't need to do all the heavy work of identifying the right direction yourself. Fortunately, there is a wealth of wisdom already out there. Enough people in history have already committed most of the mistakes and learned the necessary lesson. And the best part is that they have distilled the wisdom learned and openheartedly poured that wisdom in the form of books or other resources that are easily and also not that expensively available to everyone in the world. So you are already in a good luck living in this modern age, where most of the information is available to you with the click of a button. You don't need to go the hard route of trying everything yourself and reinvent the wheel by learning only after making many mistakes. There are readily available lessons.

"Learn from the mistakes of others. You can't live long enough to make them all yourself." ~ Eleanor Roosevelt

What is Your Definition of Success?

To ensure that your success doesn't lack fulfillment; to ensure that you don't end up feeling like a loser even after attaining your 'so called' success, you need to first be clear how would your success look like when you *reach* there.

Once you have seen that picture in your mind, only then you should start putting your efforts in that direction.

As is rightly said:

> *"Begin with the end in mind." ~ Stephen R. Covey*

Let's start with the definition of success.

The plain and simplest meaning of success as per the dictionary is "the accomplishment of an aim or purpose." Hence, the meaning of success is bound to differ from one person to other because each individual on this planet can have a different aim or purpose. Everyone has a different barometer with a separate set of parameters to measure success.

For most people, the definition of success would be achieving the financial goals, living in a house of their dreams, or driving their dream car or having fun and adventure at most exotic places or experiencing the material pleasures of this world. On the other hand, there could be people on an altogether different extreme. For a few people, success could simply mean travelling their inner journey, exploring for deeper spiritual treasure, and experiencing the stage of enlightenment or nirvana. Consider the example of Gautama

Buddha, financial success didn't matter to him at all. In fact, having been born as a prince, his future as a king of a kingdom was guaranteed at birth. This can be the height of prosperity and financial success for anyone in the world. But this financial abundance didn't mean anything for him because his definition of success was to touch the heightened stages of consciousness and enlightenment through an inner spiritual journey and nothing less than that.

For someone, self-less serving the humanity could be the yardstick for measurement of success. Consider Mother Teresa – for her, helping the less-privileged poor people to lead a better life was the only life goal and thus her definition of success. Similarly, Nelson Mandela spent a substantial portion of his life for fighting and securing the equal rights to vote for black people in South Africa. His definition of success was to win his fight against racism and create a nation with equal rights to all regardless of colour or creed.

The different examples shown above indicate that there cannot be any objective definition of success, as it differs from person to person as per his or her values in life. But one thing is sure that there are some deeper inner elements that need to definitely be addressed if one intends to live a life of success together with a sense of fulfillment.

> ***"In seeking success, you must also seek fulfillment. Ask yourself not only what you want to be but who you want to be." Elizabeth Dole***

Set Quality Goals for LASTING Success

Since the definition of success differs from person to person, our objective is to strive for such success that gives us fulfillment from inside.

Therefore, the obvious question that arises is how to ensure that one achieves success and also enjoys the gift of fulfillment. The answer lies in the finalization of your goals based on the quality of life desired from such goals. There are two categories of goals from the quality perspective and it would be beneficial to have a look at the different parameters that these goals address before we finalize our goals. Two categories of goals are as listed below:

1. Extrinsic Goals
2. Intrinsic Goals

Extrinsic Goals

Extrinsic goals are the goals which are primarily focused on the outside aspiration related to money, fame, or beauty. Each of these aspirations requires validation from the outside world. These goals help you achieve something outside of yourself. They have the metrics to define success dependent on the outside world.

They are about polishing your public image, becoming famous, getting rich, or seeking power over others. These goals are all about the prize at the end of the journey. They are more about attaining certain outcomes without focussing much or even neglecting the process involved.

Intrinsic Goals

On the other hand, intrinsic goals are all about doing or following something personally meaningful to you. These goals address your core needs and wants – who you are as a person. They pertain to your passions, interests, and core values as well as your relationships and your personal growth.

Intrinsic goals satisfy your core human needs for relatedness, competence, and autonomy. They include goals for relationships, personal growth, physical health, self-acceptance, and contribution.

Your goal is an intrinsic goal if it helps:

i. To create a stronger relationship with like-minded people or giving back to the society.
ii. To give you a sense of autonomy, i.e., it is something that is your passion or truly excites you. If no one forces you to do it and you can continue to do it for longer hours on your own, then it is an intrinsic goal.
iii. To grow you personally, i.e., if it is some skill you want to master and grow. It is something that

makes you feel that you are good at something.

To put it simply, being intrinsically motivated means doing the thing for the thing itself. It's about enjoying the doing, not just looking for the outcome.

The following could be some examples of extrinsic vs. intrinsic goals:

- Exercise to build muscles to show off to people is EXTRINSIC.
- Exercising to enjoy the feeling of fitness and vibrant health is INTRINSIC
- Studying solely for the purposes of getting grades and securing a job is EXTRINSIC
- Studying something you love exploring the subject and get deeper because you are passionate about the subject is INTRINSIC

In his book *Why We Do What We Do,* Edward L. Deci explains how intrinsic goals help to attain more happiness and enhance the quality of life and overall well-being. In his words:

"….if any of the three extrinsic aspirations—for money, fame, or beauty—was very high for an individual relative to the three intrinsic aspirations, the individual was also more likely to display poorer mental health. For example, having an unusually strong aspiration for material success was associated with narcissism, anxiety, depression, and poorer social functioning as rated by a trained clinical psychologist…

In contrast, strong aspirations for any of the intrinsic goals—meaningful relationships, personal growth, and community contributions—were positively associated with well-being. People who strongly desired to contribute to their community, for example, had more vitality and higher self-esteem. When people organize their behaviour in terms of intrinsic strivings (relative to extrinsic strivings) they seem more content—they feel better about who they are and display more evidence of psychological health."

On the other hand, extrinsic goals are associated with anxiety, depression, and a lower level of happiness. In her book, *Succeed,* author Heidi Grant Halvorson states:

"Here are the goals that aren't going to help you achieve lasting well-being: becoming famous, seeking power over others, or polishing your public image. Any goal related to obtaining other people's validation and approval or external signs of self-worth isn't going to do it for you, either. Accumulating wealth for its own sake also won't lead to real happiness (this is not to say you should care about money at all, just that being rich isn't a sure ticket to a happy life)."

The above observations are in fact confirmed by other people, and most successful people have pursued their success journey with the conscious choice of intrinsic goals. Mark Twain wisely made the below statement about the power of intrinsic goals.

> ***"The law of work seems unfair, but nothing can change it; the more enjoyment you get out of your work, the more money you will make."***

See what the titan of the investment world, Warren Buffett, has to offer. He says, "There comes a time when you ought to start doing what you want. Take a job that you love. You will jump out of bed in the morning. I think you are out of your mind if you keep taking jobs that you don't like because you think it will look good on your resume. Isn't that a little like saving up sex for your old age?"

Bill Gates, founder of Microsoft and the richest person in the world, when talking about starting Microsoft with Paul Allen, stated, "Paul and I, we never thought that we would make much money out of the thing. We just loved writing software."

Last but not least, Steve Jobs said in his infamous Stanford University commencement speech,

"You've got to find what you love. And that is as true for your work as it is for your lovers. Your work is going to fill a large part of your life, and the only way to be truly satisfied is to do what you believe is great work. And the only way to do great work is to love what you do. If you haven't found it yet, keep looking. Don't settle. As with all matters of the heart, you'll know when you find it. And, like any great relationship, it just gets better and better as the years roll on. So keep looking until you find it. Don't settle…"

But the irony is that despite being nudged by our consciousness to move towards the real goals in our lives, we keep on moving towards the extrinsic goals. Again, it is worth referring to the book *Succeed*, where Heidi Grant Halvorson's explains the precise reasons for that:

"Psychologists Deci and Ryan argue that we turn to these superficial goals, these external sources of self-worth, when our needs for autonomy, relatedness, and competence are thwarted again and again. This can happen when we find ourselves trapped in situations that are too controlling (robbing us of our sense of personal freedom), over-challenging (robbing us of our sense of competence), or rejecting (robbing us of our sense of relatedness). In other words, when we are under too much pressure or denied choices, when we feel we can't do anything right, and when we are lonely and lack meaningful relationships with others, we turn to goals that aren't very good for us as a kind of defensive strategy. "If I can't get the love I need in my life, then I'll become rich and famous and people will love me for that." The irony and tragedy of this strategy is that the pursuit of fame, wealth, and popularity pretty much guarantees that your basic needs aren't going to be met. These goals are lousy substitutes for the goals we really should be pursuing. They'll keep you busy but never make you truly happy."

Therefore, in order to have a lasting happiness and to lead a life of joy and fulfillment, one needs to be introspective and choose the goals for intrinsic reasons and not run solely on the extrinsic factors to avoid repenting at later stages.

Short-Term Project Vs. Long-Term Goal

Now after knowing the distinction between extrinsic and intrinsic goals and realizing the significance of intrinsic goals for our well-being, let's examine one more element about the longevity or duration of the goals we set for ourselves.

You'd have noticed that most people talk about setting up long-term goals. They tell us to prepare your life goals and then break these down into your ten-year goal. We then have to break it down to a five-years goal, and then a further short-term goal, i.e., one-year goal. The idea is to design your life for a far longer period and then break it down into shorter period goals.

This seems a good approach, as you feel aligned yourself aligned with your life purpose. But, there is one drawback to this approach, as you will use your current level of consciousness or wisdom attained and plan out your entire life based on that. In this approach, you cannot take into account enhancement in your thinking capacities or unfolding of future circumstances in your life that may pose the even better prospects and opportunities to lead a life.

The reason I am stating the above is that I heard of some unconventional approach to the periodicity of goals setting through a selection of shorter term projects instead of long-term goals.

In an interview with Tony Robbins, best-selling author of multiple books, Tim Ferriss states that when he stated his career, he used to make longer term goals as most people do, but now he focuses on working for shorter projects for say six months to say maximum one-year duration. He doesn't decide his goals for too long of a period. The underlying principle behind this strategy, as he explained, is that based on the current level of his expertise, competence, and his worldview, it is best suited to just work on some project with 100% dedication and then wait for what unfolds in front of him.

He says this approach takes into account the new facts or life circumstances that unfold because of the current short-term projects being pursued. This approach helps to avoid the rigidity associated with the longer-term goals. With that approach, he thinks he may explore much larger and much better possibilities that may arise solely as a result of the ongoing project.

Personally, I also believe this to be a better approach. It is because, sitting at today, if you have to make your life goal or ten-year goal, that goal would be set up totally on the basis of your current level of understanding and your limited worldview based on your present intelligence. But if you compare this to a one-year project, you would be able to better draw your plans or project for one year. In that one-year period, you enhance your worldview, meet more people, build better connections, enhance your mind's reference fabric by exposing it to a variety of experiences, and then you are ready to make another assessment of your life.

The best part is you are making yourself flexible in approach. You are also allowing the life to unfold to you and then based on the feedback from life experiences; you can structure or re-structure your plans for better.

You would appreciate that the objective of stating the different approaches towards setting up your goal was to give you a broader perspective before you venture into your success journey. This wider perspective will help you to carefully choose your goals to reap the sustainable rewards for a lifetime. Your goals consume your life and you must be sure about the reward before putting your precious life to something.

In the nutshell, the best goal for you should be that which makes you feel you have evolved and mastered your life. Because:

"What you get by achieving your goals is not as important as what you become by achieving your goals." ~ Zig Ziglar

Get Your Toolbox for the Success Journey

This book is about not only achieving success but also being able to enjoy and lead a life of joy and fulfillment. After elaborate discussions on success, fulfillment, and goals and explaining the principles about what goals should deserve your time, now I offer the later sections of this book as a toolbox to accompany on your journey towards the true success. This toolbox will help you keep sharpening your inner capabilities and help you stay on the path of your chosen goals fully equipped with the right set of mental tools.

You can compare your journey to success to climbing a mountain. The path to success is not like driving on the plain road. Had it been a plain road, then everyone would have been successful, and you wouldn't have heard about huge percentage people failing. It is often stated in the world of entrepreneurship that out of 100 new businesses starting every year, more than 95% get wound up in the first five years of their setting up. Do you know why?

It is because reaching the top of the mountain requires adequate training, appropriate tools, and mental stamina to stick to the journey in the face of cold and strong winds, arduous and life-threatening paths, and consistent fear of not being able to make it or even losing all you have. You cannot simply just start climbing the mountain without any preparation, training or required accessories.

Think about what kind of tools you would need for your physical journey to the mountain. You need to have proper footwear, crampons, rope, harness, etc. with you to climb the mountain and stay safe. Then you need to be physically and mentally strong enough to continue that journey despite the difficulties coming on your way. You need to have a certain amount of training before you take the leap of faith and start your journey.

Therefore, we need to treat our journey to success like climbing a mountain. You need to be equipped with mental tools of persistence, faith, and a strong desire to achieve your goals. You need to have the requisite resources in the form of money, time, and support from your mentors to keep you focused and moving towards your goals. In this book, I have captured the relevant mental tools and necessary strategies to help you not to drift from your course and keep moving towards your goals in a focused manner.

Let me briefly explain what this book will offer to you. In this book:

- ➤ You will learn about the meaning of true success and how should you move ahead to determine your life goals for a long-term success and fulfillment without compromising on your happiness and overall well-being.

- ➤ You will discover the importance of and how to determine your true identity in order to unleash your potential and gear up your action to the next level.

- ➤ You will learn the four different zones into which all your human activities fall. These activities start from an unrewarding zone of incompetence activities and range to the life-changing zone of genius activities essential to lead a fulfilling and extremely rewarding life.

➢ One full section will explain to you the significance of three 'S's of the term Success and how these three 'S's are necessary to keep you in the right frame of mind that enables you to always feel motivated and thriving to keep taking massive actions towards your dreams.

➢ Last but not least, you will discover some less heard but highly effective sharp mental tools that super achievers already use and how can you develop these mental tools to face the tough winds of life and come out thriving.

I assure you that by the time you finish reading this book, your mind will be already be craving to jump to the immediate next action towards your life goals. This book promises to equip you with essential tools to help you get maximum clarity about who you are and what your goals are, followed by a massive action towards achieving your goals.

With that, let's immediately start our next section to ascertain who you really are and how that clarity will help you to give an exponential pace towards your goals.

So let's get going…

PART II: "You" Are the Starting Point of Your Success Journey

******

"Our lives improve only when we take chances—and the first and most difficult risk we can take is to be honest with ourselves." ~ Walter Anderson

Embrace Your Identity

It is a well-known principle that before you venture into any of your big goals, you need to clarify your *why* – an unshakeable *why*, i.e., definiteness of purpose. Your 'whys' are an indicator of what your values and priorities in life are. Only if your *why* is strong enough will it make you entirely immersed in the pursuit of achieving your objective.

Undoubtedly, a strong *why* is a big motivator for you to fast track your progress, but there is another very important element of the game and without that, you can't exhibit your full potential into your venture. It is identifying your deeper personal identity – it is to know and claim who you are. Because:

> ***"Your identity precedes your activity."***

While your *whys* are your reasons for choosing any activity or pursuit, who you determine yourself to be leads you to take massive action that leads to mastery in your chosen field. It is who you identify yourself as that triggers you to take actions based on the standards of that identity.

If you are a CEO of a company and also attach that identity to yourself – you find yourself responsible for the results of your company, you make yourself accountable for the well-being of your employees to pay their wages. By owning that identity to your deep self, you take actions that a CEO ought to take for the growth of the company. Only if you are sincerely attached to your identity as a CEO will you be bothered about the minute details of all the plans of your company, you will be dedicated to delivering excellence. Any results less than the best will prompt you to improve your game.

If you are a professional, i.e., an accountant, a lawyer, or an architect, and you believe in your identity beyond doubt, then your actions will be uniquely filled with passion. A writer needs to claim in mind and heart his identity as a writer before he is able to start generating quality work and master his craft. With that identity, he is not very far from the day when people become his true fans and reward him by purchasing every product he creates.

But if someone doesn't love his work and is unable to identify himself in that role, he is surely on the path of mediocrity and ultimately will lead to failure. Claiming your identity is the first step before you are able to generate any quality work and leave your mark of excellence. And that's the true path to create harmony and happiness in your life.

> *"Happiness is when, what you think, what you say and what you do, are in harmony."*
> *~ Mahatma Gandhi*

Some schools of thought suggest that one should not be grossly attached to one's identity. This is because if you fail in your endeavours, it will feel as if *you* are a failure. Many spiritual teachings, including Buddhism, state that attachment is the reason for all suffering. But Brendon Burchard, in his book *High Performance Habits,* writes that one has to be so connected with his true identity before he or she could do anything significant. He suggests that you have to go 'all in' to create something magical out of your abilities.

Einstein once rightly stated:

> ***"Only one who devotes himself to a cause with his whole strength and soul can be a true master. For this reason, mastery demands all of a person." Albert Einstein***

Gandhi changed his identity in his mind from being a lawyer to a freedom fighter.

One incident of being ousted due to his black colour, from a train compartment reserved for white people, made him choose a larger-than-life goal – freeing his country India from British rule. Once he chose that identity, then all his actions emanated from that identity. Gandhi's attachment with his identity as a freedom fighter for the country enabled him to instil a sense of faith in more than two-hundred million people of India to believe in his vision of independent country with his philosophy of non-violence.

People who have succeeded massively in any venture are those who have forced themselves "all in" with their chosen identity before they could achieve anything significant. So the first principle is to make yours a firm identity of who you are and how with that identity you can serve the humanity with your full potential.

How do you get clear about your identity?

Identifying your true self is so crucial to your success, but still, most people spend their entire life hiding something in their hearts and don't open up. This is because often there is such a huge mixture of thoughts and emotions in our mind and bodies that it becomes very difficult to really get a hold of who we truly are.

But the key thing here is to realize that you and only you can determine who you are. Nobody from outside can tell you your true identity. Outside people may help you trigger some leading questions, but you and you only need to find out the answers from deep within.

So what should you do to get clear about who you are?

I learned a simple strategy from Jesse Elder, a business advisor and personal development coach, and found it very powerful for activating your intuition to seek inner cues. You can do it right now as well, if you are at home or at the office, and it will just take two minutes.

Stand in front of the mirror. Ensure that there are no distractions or disturbances. Set a timer for 2 minutes on your mobile. Now look into your eyes with deep emotions of love and kindness towards yourself. Now start asking "Who am I?" Not once, not twice, but the entire duration of two minutes slowly and slowly. When you ask this question, keep looking into your eyes in the mirror and simultaneously observe any thoughts in your mind and emotions in your body. After this session, just sit silently for 5 minutes with a pen and paper. Some thoughts will pop up in your head and most probably these are the signals from the universe or infinite intelligence answering your repeated question. Now it is your job to capture those answers.

Follow this practice for one week on a daily basis along with 5 minutes of silent sitting.

You will be amazed at the results. Don't go by my words, just try on your own – it is powerful. You will be amazed by the real powers available within us to guide and lead us in the right direction to make the best out of our lives.

Are You Obsessed or Just Passionate?

> ***"Success is your duty, obligation, and responsibility."* - *Grant Cardone***

Grant Cardone is the author of the best-selling book, *Be Obsessed or Be Average*, and many other best-selling books. Besides being a New York Times best-selling author, Grant is an internationally renowned speaker on leadership, real estate investing, entrepreneurship, and finance. He has five privately held companies that have annual revenues exceeding $100 million and holds a portfolio of over 3,800 apartment units throughout the U.S. with transactions valued at over $500 million[4].

Why I am stating Grant's credentials.? Because in *Be Obsessed or Be Average*, he tells his personal grand success story and gives the entire credit of his success to his obsession with his work. He states that his journey from a lost and broken twenty-five-year-old young man to a successful business owner was possible only through the power of obsession.

Now read his quote again and you will immediately sense if someone considers achieving success to be your duty, obligation, and responsibility, he can't state so unless he is obsessed with success.

Also, Brendon Burchard, author of the best-selling book *High Performance Habits* states that merely being passionate is not

---

[4] https://www.amazon.com/Grant-Cardone/e/B0038X6X5W/

going to cut the ice, rather, you must be obsessed with what you do.

There is a thin line between passion and obsession. In passion, you get engaged in activities which you enjoy and find that activity important and therefore spend a considerable amount of time doing that activity. Obsession also has similar features. But one difference is that in passion, you do everything out of your free will. You can start and stop what you're doing whenever you choose to stop, whereas in obsession, the work you enjoy catches you and supersedes everything else. And that's where the magic happens as you are able to generate a massive output.

From a societal standpoint, you are passionate when people praise you for spending time on the things you love, and they generally talk positively about it. But obsession is the stage when people may start calling you crazy or a maniac, because you start operating from a level beyond the normal standards of society – now you don't care about what people will think or say about you, because you just keep doing what you are obsessed with.

Similarly, Price Pritchett, a business advisor in merger, culture, and organization changes, and consultant to major Fortune 100 companies, in his best-selling book *You Squared: A High Velocity Formula for Multiplying Your Personal Effectiveness in Quantum Leaps* explains the principles of achievement success by taking a quantum leap. One of the key ingredients for a quantum leap success is to identify your magnetic aiming point – a goal you want to pursue with obsession. Your goal should be such that it engulfs you entirely and consume you – It can't be a normal goal, it must be your obsession.

Since obsession is the key to massive action and therefore to produce massive results; therefore, it becomes all the more significant to choose your goals cautiously, as explained in the previous section, and then only be obsessed about achieving that goal.

Look around the world and you will notice that all magnificently successful people in the world were deeply obsessed with their work or craft.

Steve Jobs was obsessed with the design and seamless operation of phones and thus created the world's most enviable touch screen smart phones.

Elon Musk is filled with an obsession to do larger-than-life things like setting up a colony on Mars and making travel between any part of the world less than an hour through space rockets, etc.

Tony Robbins, Robin Sharma, Brendon Burchard, the topmost names in the personal development industry, are deeply in love to the level of obsession with their craft and mission to inspire the world to live an impactful life.

All these people are highly obsessed with their work and not merely passionate about it. They have already devoted their life to their obsession for their craft so deeply that it is strenuously integrated with their ultimate mission. With such an obsession, you can't ever have a thought of quitting or going back – you just keep moving ahead consistently, whether it is a day or night, summer or winter, rain or sun.

As is rightly said,

> ***"When you want something, all the universe conspires in helping you to achieve it." - Paulo Coelho***

When you are totally immersed in something you enjoy and feel is important, then you never realize how much time you are spending on it. It feels like being with your beloved – and who cares about time when you are totally immersed in that other human being? When you are obsessed, this is not a work at all. That's why Confucius aptly stated, *"Choose a job you love, and you will never have to work a day in your life."*

Work, by definition, means an activity involving mental or physical effort done in order to achieve a result. By when you love something or someone, then it means that you are doing that thing not for any extraneous result or reward to follow later, rather you are getting an instant reward in the form of inner satisfaction and fulfillment by the very thing or the person you love. You are doing it for the sake of doing it and not for any other future reasons or results. There is no waiting period between the work and the results, in case you are obsessed with the work. The instant reward is in doing the work itself.

For example, if you do a day job that you don't like, then you are doing that job with a specific objective of getting paid for that activity. With that feeling, you are just trying to fill that time of 9 to 5 with the bare minimum necessary for you to survive in that job. The end result you expect from that work is your wages at the end of the month. But if you like the work you do. You don't feel like someone is exploiting you to get his or her work done.

It would be appropriate to share here one example from my earlier consulting days. It is about the approach of one young lawyers' obsession with getting deeper into legal intricacies. His curiosity to get clarity on and obsession for finding solutions on complex legal issues was so deep that he didn't care about what the time was. At times I found him in the office in critical meetings offering his opinion on complex legal matters in the morning. And surprisingly enough before such discussions, he had burned the midnight oil to explore everything about the subject and had gone home at 4 a.m. that day. His uncanny obsession made him consistently read dozens of lengthy court judgments, each ranging from fifty to a few hundred pages at night.

No one forced him ever to sit the long nights in the office to do that research. Even some senior colleagues in the firm had a tendency to simply approach this young man to find the solution to complex legal problems. But this young man didn't show a flinch of feeling exploited, because he was obsessed with his work. Also, he knew the kind of obsession he has for the finer details about his work would make him a specialist and indispensable asset of the firm. Today, he enjoys an enviable senior position in the firm, thanks to his obsession with the work.

Therefore, once you are clear about your inner deeper reasons or 'whys'; have claimed your identity; and assured yourself that your goals will lead you to success with fulfillment, it is time to get obsessed with your work, which will put you on a path towards faster success.

In future sections, you will learn about various mental tools and strategies to leverage your strengths that will give you an exponential edge over others to achieve your goals faster. However, in the immediate next section, you will learn the different zones of activities; you get engaged in your work day and how you need to keep moving towards your ultimate zone of genius to truly live a fulfilled life.

PART III: Your Four Activity Zones and How to Reach Your Top Zone

****

> *"What we think or what we know or what we believe is, in the end, of little consequence. The only consequence is what we do." ~ John Ruskin*

In the previous sections, we have talked at a broad level about your definition of success and how you should choose your goals to lead a life of fulfillment along with success. Then we moved ahead more specifically about you, your identity, and finally the power of obsession with whatever you do to attain a massive success.

This section is about enhancing your awareness about the activities you engaged yourself in. The objective of this section is to safeguard your precious time from being wasted on low-priority activities and find out your most important activities that will lead you towards the ultimate path of fulfillment.

I learnt from Gay Hendricks about the four zones in which all your activities get categorized through his book, *The Big Leap*. It is very important to analyse on what activities you are spending your time, whether it is the right utilization of your time, and if you need to make any changes in your approach, so you can lead the best quality of your life. Following are the four zones in which all are activities could be categorised.

    a. Zone of Incompetence
    b. Zone of Competence
    c. Zone of Excellence
    d. Zone of Genius.

Let's understand the activities that get categorized into the different zones as below:

1. Zone of Incompetence

As the name itself suggest, the zone of incompetence covers those activities we are not good at. There are other people who can do it much better than us. An example will explain the activities falling under this zone.

John purchased a new four-wheeler last week. As it generally happens when you get something new, he is very excited about his new possession, his dream car. However, over the weekend, he finds a red colour light blinking on the odometer when he was driving the car to the supermarket. He reached home and was curious to know why this light continued to blink. He opens the manual of the vehicle, and reads through the relevant pages and somehow realizes that there is some minor fixing needed in the car batteries. Now, notice he is not a car mechanic. Rather, he is a management consultant, and he proudly charges up to five hundred dollars per hour as his consultancy fees from his clients.

But somehow, he is very excited and determined to fix this car problem on his own. He goes to his garage, opens the car bonnet, and starts casually fiddling with the various wires around the car batteries. After following some directions in the car manual, which he vaguely understood, he now checks the car, but the problem persists. He again tries, still not succeeding. He ends up spending 4–5 hours of his time trying to fix something, in which he is not competent. Finally, he calls up a neighbourhood car mechanic and shows the problem to him. The car mechanic opens the bonnet and within next 15 minutes, he fixes the problem by connecting the right wiring in the car batteries. The issue got resolved and John paid just a paltry amount of thirty dollars to the mechanic for his service.

Now you can see, being a management consultant, whose time's value is five hundred dollars per hour, John is not supposed to know how to fix the car. But only to prove to himself that he can do it or maybe to save a few bucks, he wasted five hours of his weekend time. And adding to the woes, he had a fight with his wife that day, as he could not get her and the family to the latest movie that evening.

This is a perfect example that John was operating in his zone of incompetence and thus ended up wasting his precious time on things that didn't deserve his time.

You may also want to assess your life to verify if you have been engaged in some activities that lie in the zone of incompetence given your circumstances. If you realize that you also sometime waste time in the zone of incompetence, keep reading for a solution.

How should you handle the zone of incompetence?

It is rather straightforward. You must make a decision to never engage in any activity that is in your zone of incompetence. Rather, you should immediately delegate such activity to someone else who is competent to address that activity.

This principle applies to those areas entirely beyond the scope of your work. However, if the work relates to some area which you are interested in learning and growing in that area, that's an entirely different ballgame.

Assuming you are a corporate lawyer – if there is some new area of practice evolving in which you find yourself interested – and you think there is a scope to grow, then this should not be avoided in the guise of stating it as your zone of incompetence.

This activity would fall outside your comfort zone (but it is not in your zone of incompetence) and if it helps to sharpen your skills, you should be learning and doing this additional activity. Here we are talking about only those activities that don't relate to your key skills and don't generate value for your time spent, hence get covered in the zone of incompetence. Therefore, the best course of action is that one should get rid of such activities at the soonest possible. Hendricks calls involvement in those activities as *"stuck on stupid,"* but also makes an exception, stating that it is worthwhile to do something you're not good at only if the intention is to enjoy or master it, i.e., skiing, yoga teaching.

With that, let's move to the next zone.

2. Zone of Competence

This zone covers those activities, in which you are good at. But you also realize that any other person can also do it as good as you do. The problem with carrying out only these activities (and nothing beyond) is that the longer you do it, you will start feeling yourself suffering from a disease of unfulfillment. And most successful people find themselves engaged in doing such things which others can do just as well. Then why don't they simply delegate it to others?

It is because they think it would be a hassle to first delegate the work to someone and then to follow up with that person. It seems to them they can do it faster if they do it on their own. No doubt, it doesn't make them dependent on someone outside, but that time they could have spent on something which would matter them more.

In an interview, Rory Vaden, author of best-selling book *Procrastinate on Purpose,* suggested that you should be willing to spend 30X the time it takes you to do an activity in training someone to do it for you. For example, if it takes five minutes for you to input some information into your software every day, you should be ready to spend up to two and half hours (150 minutes) to teach someone to do it for you. It may seem like spending too much on training someone, so better you do it yourself. Yes, it seems a bit of concern from a short-term perspective. But in reality, you will get a long-term ROTI (return on time invested), because after thirty days (you will recover your original time invested in thirty days) you will still continue to save your time doing that activity for a long term. The saved time can be utilized for something more productive and rewarding.

If you can do something on your own, that doesn't mean you should continue to do so if it is not your core activity and doesn't help you grow faster.

What is the right way to get out of this zone of competence?

It requires asking yourself a question, *"If you could stop those activities in the zone of competence, what would it free up time for you to do? If money or job description were not an issue what would you really like to be doing?"*

With enough asking, you will get to hear some inner voice eventually guiding you to take some action.

Hendricks gives an example of his coaching client, who was good at organizing events, managing the calendar, or fixing any meetings in her organization. But as she competently handled those activities, she was given more and more of such activities. Over a time, she started getting a feeling of chronic fatigue. Hendricks states this problem sometimes as "diseases of unfulfillment." He states that when people are not able to express their full potential, they often get caught by some diseases that have vague and hard-to-diagnose symptoms. Upon questioning, this woman realized that if she had enough time, she would love to work on one environment revival project, which had been in the back of her mind for so many years. But she was worried about how she could be able to make a living out of the work that fulfills her. Finally, she started taking steps to improve her life and to move out of her zone of competence to higher levels. She stopped taking additional mundane work from colleagues that was beyond her scope of work and also started delegating her work to other people as much as possible. Within few weeks her symptoms of chronic fatigue started to disappear. Finally, she was able to cut back her office timing to half by having a discussion with the company and devoting more time to her environment project she wanted to work on.

Therefore, it's a time for you to examine if you are spending too much time on your zone of competence and ask yourself the same question, *"What would you love to spend time upon if you could stop doing activities in the zone of competence?"*

With that, let's now move to the next zone of activities called the zone of excellence.

3. Zone of Excellence

The name of this zone apparently attracts and moreover seems to suggest that you have arrived and therefore you can stay here for life (but, wait until you read the next one). The activities covered in this zone are the activities which you do extremely well and also, you make a good living in this zone.

This is the zone where your own addiction to comfort wants you to stay. Moreover, your family, friends, and relatives want you to stay in this zone as well. You are reliable there, and you easily provide a steady supply of things on which your family, friends, and relationships thrive on.

For successful people, this zone is quite seductive and even a dangerous trap. Why? It is because this zone stops successful people from moving from good to great. Though you excel in a particular field and make a great living out of it, there is still some inner voice nagging in your head, which can be called your true calling. The problem with staying in this zone of excellence is that a deeper and sacred part of you will start dying slowly if you remain here. Therefore, the question comes, what comes next after being excellent.

Hendricks suggests that there is only one place where you will ultimately thrive and feel satisfied and that place is called "Zone of Genius." Let's talk about this final and ultimately rewarding zone now.

4. Zone of Genius

This is the zone where you feel liberating and are expressing your natural genius towards your ultimate path to success and fulfillment. This zone comprises those activities which you are uniquely suited to do. These are your special gifts or abilities, which the world can benefit from. You have a deeper sense of pulling towards doing these activities as you grow up, which Hendricks termed as a *'call to genius.'* Hendricks further states that by the age of forty, most of us 'tune out' the call to genius and the resultant symptoms are increasing anxiety, depressions, illness, or relationship conflicts, etc. These symptoms are the alarms which keep on telling us we need to pay attention to what matters most to us. These alarms prompt us to feed our natural genius and let our inner genius spread the magic to the world.

It is recommended that we should heed the call to genius in a gentle and graceful manner. Because if we don't pay attention to it, sometimes life gives us shocking jolts that tell us with blatant clarity that we are not paying attention to the call to genius.

Hendricks explains his tragic personal experience with one of the clients, who seemingly ignored his call to genius for a long time. Read the excerpt from *The Big Leap* below:

"I recall a coaching conversation with Bill, a brilliant forty-three-year-old entrepreneur, who had been turning a deaf ear to his Call to Genius for far too long. He came in for one session, in which he told me about the bind he was in. Bill wanted passionately to pursue a certain new project, but he said he couldn't do it because of pressure from his company, his wife, and others. He said they could not afford to have him take the several months necessary to work on the new idea. As he described the new project, I could tell it was clearly in his Zone of Genius. I counselled Bill to do whatever it took to make it happen, even if he could spend only an hour a day laying the groundwork for it. At the end of the session, he told me he was going to "try" to find that hour a day, but I could tell by the look on his face that it was unlikely to occur.

He told me he would call me in a month to schedule a second appointment "when things slowed down a little." It was our last conversation, because Bill died of a massive heart attack a few weeks later.

I have replayed that hour with him in my mind more times than I can count. Bill was seemingly in perfect health. His wife was a yoga teacher; they were both devoted to a healthy lifestyle. I've always wondered if there was a way in which I could have been more forceful with him in helping him make a life-changing, and possibly life-saving, commitment to his Zone of Genius."

This is a shocking example showing the tragic end of a seemingly successful career (from the perspective of the outside world), because of failing to pay close attention to inner cues towards a call to genius.

Hendricks further goes on to state that with the right tools and a little wisdom, we can start to listen through intuition and react to the call to genius – and that will save us from all the suffering and pain that arises from neglecting the inner voices. He recommends that one should be aiming to spend seventy percent of his time in the activities in the zone of genius to lead a life of fulfillment and true success.

In my view, *The Big Leap* by Hendricks has the potential to offer you the right tool to ascertain your zone of genius activities and how you can start moving towards that starting by merely spending ten minutes a day to start with.

Therefore, consider this section of the book as an assessment sheet to examine the activities that consume your days. If you are not moving towards your zone of genius activities, then it is the time to pay close attention to your inner voice and start spending time in the activities falling in your zone of genius. The last section of this book will equip you with various tools that will help you listen to your inner subtle cues calling you toward your genius, so stay tuned.

Now we will learn about the 3Ss of Success in next section.

PART IV: Harness the Power of Three 'S's in SUCCESS & Optimize Your Performance

****

> *"Success is a state of mind. If you want success, start thinking of yourself as a success." - Joyce Brothers*

So far, you have learned about the significance of setting up well thought out and quality goals from a holistic perspective to achieve success with fulfillment. We also dived deeper into the importance of claiming and living your true identity and how obsession can help you achieve big goals. In the previous section, we got into details about why you should listen to the call to genius and move to your zone of genius, leaving other zones behind.

Everything sounds good so far. And these are definitely the right set of principles and lay the right foundation to start creating a monumental life. But there is still something that needs to be addressed to progress seamlessly without any inner conflicts on a moment to moment basis. You'd have noticed that often, despite doing everything right, there are times when you don't feel like moving ahead. You realize that there is something inside that is pulling you backwards and you realize that you are not moving ahead faster.

This section will help you learn the core inner principles of life that will keep you in the perfect state of mind most of the time – a state where you become unstoppable. Let me clarify one thing precisely here and I have often been in such situations.

So, if you are like me, you would have found yourself in such a heightened state of your mind that you think like you deserve everything in the world and therefore you can do anything to achieve your big goals. But maybe a few hours or a few days after you start taking action, you find yourself plagued with some negative thought or fear of a negative outcome.

Though, when you are in the heightened state of your mind, you feel sad that you had wasted your time in doubting yourself and your capabilities. This sadness comes, because you realize that had you been able to maintain a heightened state for a longer period of time, you could have taken massive action towards fulfillment of your ambitions You know that your consistent effort and massive actions inspired by such a heightened state of mind starts showing result in a short time, as the principle of compound effect comes into play.

But ironically, if you continuously keep swinging like a pendulum between that heightened state and then drift to your lowest self, this is the worst thing you are doing to yourself. You are punishing yourself and pushing yourself to remain in the state of mediocrity. If someone believes he is not good enough, his mind operates on the level of mediocrity. He can't think of flying high because his belief system doesn't allow him to think beyond a certain level – beyond the imaginary limit he has set for himself.

The longer we allow ourselves to fluctuate between the heightened stage and the low self-esteem stage, the more it starts denting our confidence. We start doubting and second-guessing ourselves. The journey of dreamers is a lonely journey because for the majority of the population dreaming is like an ailment and they use all precautions to not get bitten by this insect called 'dream.'

So what's the deal here? How do we achieve a state in which we keep on consistently performing?

That's we will cover in this section of the book. In fact, the objective of this section is to ensure that dreamers continuously stay in the periods of heightened awareness and in a productive state and further maximise such period for longer periods to reap the benefits. The more a dreamer can remain in the heightened state of mind, the more he will achieve and that will boost his confidence. Each action leads to boosting confidence and confidence further motivates you to take further action, so you get into a circle of positivity.

This section explains the three elements necessary for reaching and maintaining ourselves at that heightened state in our lives, which Tony Robbins explained in one of his conferences. Let's give it the name '3Ss' to Success. Incidentally, the word Success itself has 3Ss in it. All the three Ss are collectively important for everlasting success, but if we look at each 'S' individually, there is a certain degree of importance for each.

Let's understand those 3Ss individually in the reverse order of significance. They are:

1. Strategy
2. Story
3. State

We will now go deeper into each of the 3Ss below:

1. **Strategy**

The first S, i.e., Strategy, is one of the most important factors for bringing success to people's life. Big corporations live on strategies. Sometimes a few strategies are just minor tweaks in the big game that garner bigger results. You would be surprised to know that in the online marketing world, the simplest strategy of changing the colour of the "Buy Button" from black to golden can have the impact of doubling the conversion or sales numbers. We see all the time companies just change the packaging of their product or release a new advertisement of the existing product and that rewards them with an increase in revenue and profits.

Let's understand what is a strategy? Strategy means simply *"a plan of action designed to achieve a long-term or overall aim."* Of course, a good strategy gives a competitive advantage over the competitors and one can have an advantage over the other merely by following the strategies. Therefore, one must be never hesitant to invest money for learning better strategies, as smaller tweaks in your approach help you progress faster.

But strategy alone without the other two Ss of Success doesn't work at all. This is because strategy is an outward process and before that one needs to master the two other Ss, which is an internal process. Of course, if you have a good strategy, then you will have an edge over someone who has adopted a bad strategy. Strategies are very important and can make a huge difference, but not alone; you have to first master the other two elements.

Tony Robbins once said:

> ***"Success in life is 80% psychology and 20% mechanics."***

Therefore, let's understand the next 'S,' i.e., 'story.'

2. Story

By story, we mean the stories we have created by consistently running thoughts based on our past experiences or other people's opinions. And we keep on playing these stories in our minds frequently. Some articles report that the human mind runs on an average sixty thousand thoughts in a day. That's quite a big number, but more than ninety-five percent of these thoughts are just the repetition of a few thoughts.

The ingredients of these stories can be resourceful or unrewarding depending upon the kind of past experience interaction with our environment. You may ask about how our internal stories can help or disrupt the attainment of the stage of consistent motivation and progress?

Below process flow explains how our inner story can ultimately impact our action and thus results.

Stories >> Thoughts >> Feelings>> Action>> Results

The story you allow to run in your heads puts a direct impact on your thinking process. If you have a disempowering story about your past, it will create the disempowering thoughts, which will create unproductive feelings of pessimism, sadness. Now you can easily guess the kind of action one can take with such feelings.

Most of the times, in such a negative state of mind due to a negative story, you end up doing nothing but sitting on your couch watching Netflix for hours.

Note that I stated that *you allow the stories to run in your head.* I wish to put emphasis on this. Napoleon Hill in his famous book, *Think and Grow Rich,* states that the Universe has gifted every human being with consciousness and through that gift of consciousness you can very well observe and thus control your thoughts. But the irony is only a very few exercises control what goes on in their mind.

> ***"You are today where your thoughts have brought you; you will be tomorrow where your thoughts take you." ~James Allen***

Our minds can be compared to a garden and if you let it remain unattended, then weeds will grow in the garden on their own. Therefore, you have to act as a caretaker of the garden of your mind. Instead of allowing the weeds of negativity to grow, you have to take steps to grow the fruits of positive thinking and productivity.

Therefore, mastering and correcting your story is more important than the strategy. If the story in your head is of negativity, you can't even imagine applying any strategy.

With that, now let's talk about last but most important 'S' for your journey to success.

3. State

The state is nothing but your present condition or state of mind. Only in your present condition will you put things into action. If you are not in the right state of mind at any given point of time, you will not take any action. Your state is your existing level of energy and your inspiration that can either prompt you to take action or make you sit idle and do nothing in the present moment.

You can understand why State of mind comes at the top in terms of significance out of all three Ss of your journey. You can have a repository of the best of the strategies; you might be running the best story in your mind, but if you are not able to get into the right state of mind in the present moment, nothing will move. Therefore, the most important element is how you maintain your current state of being at any given point in time.

You have to work on bringing yourself in the right state from moment to moment at the top priority – right state of body and the right state of your mind. Your body needs to be in the optimal stage through proper diet and exercise that generates energy; also, your mind needs to be releasing enough dopamine, serotonin, and other helpful chemicals to immediately put you into that state of action. Only the resourceful state of your being will trigger the right actions towards achieving success.

If you achieve the right state, this will start changing your story about yourself in some time. This is because your past is consistently generated based on the actions you are taking in the present. If you are living well in the present moment, then if you look back, you are continuously creating a better past for you. With the right state of being, you will become more resourceful to take better action that leads to better results.

The Strategies will work wonders with your right story and right state of being. And all this will add up and form a continuous circle of positivity in your life. To conclude, it starts from within, but once it comes from inside strongly, it helps to leapfrog your progress if outer strategies are added to the process.

****

PART V: Effective Ways to Level-Up Your Mental Game & Accelerate Your Success

> *"Success is a matter of understanding and religiously practicing specific, simple habits that always lead to success."* ~ Robert J. Ringer

I welcome you to this section with a hope that the previous sections have helped you to look at your definition of success and ascertain the quality of your goals towards a journey of success with fulfillment. By now, you would have already realized how your internal stories have the power to accelerate your progress, if handled well or entirely stop you from moving any further if not addressed properly. You now know very well the importance of being in the perfect state so you can keep on taking right action with full energy.

This section is targeted to equip you with certain success principles that will strengthen your mental muscles and help you move faster towards your goals. The tools, you are going to learn now onwards have already been used by high achievers to master their internal state and to remain always in a state to continue to take inspired action. These tools have the potential to sharpen your mental faculties, enhance your decision-making abilities and be more resourceful – and enhanced capabilities offer the perfect framework to put massive action in a laser focused manner to bring the massive results in one's life.

So let's have a look at these mental tools:

1. Develop High Leverage Thinking

The first principle that differentiates the incredibly successful individuals from the normal human beings is their capability of high-leverage thinking.

What does high-leverage thinking mean?

Let's understand this with the help of a simple example. Assume there is a large heavy stone lying on the ground that you want to move to some distance. Now if you simply try to push that heavy stone with your hands or other parts of the body; you will find it an extremely arduous activity to shift that stone even with your hardest efforts. But there is a different way of handling this activity. You can take a strong and thick steel rod or bar, put that rod under the heavy stone from one side to work as a lever and push it. Now you will see that it was comparatively much easier to make that rock move from its place. Why did that difficult and arduous activity became easier merely by using some iron rod?

It is because, in the latter scenario, you have used the iron rod as a 'lever' and therefore used the power of 'leverage' to shift the heavy stone. That one iron rod, if used properly as a lever, has the power to move heavier objects.

Now let's have a look at another regular scenario in our life. Every human being has the same twenty-four hours during the day. But we all know not everyone is able to generate the same amount of value out of those hours. If someone is working to earn say 50,000$ in one year, then by putting more sincere efforts and doing hard work, he may earn a 100,000 $ in one year. But as you keep progressing in your life, the rule of more hard work and generating more money through merely your hard work stop working. It is not possible for anyone to work ten times as much to start earning 500,000$. You cannot work for 400 hours (instead of forty hours) in a week, because that is not possible, as your week has only 168 hours.

The ratio between the time put versus the returns generated out of that time become extremely disproportionate if you tend to look at the numbers of billionaires. As per a survey conducted by Wealth-X[5] in the year 2013, Warren Buffett made $12.7 billion in the year 2013 – that means $37 million per day and $1.54 million per hour. The Survey states that Bill Gates earned $11.5 billion that year, which works out to be $33.3 million per day or $1.38 million per hour.

How have these people been able to earn such huge sums of money despite having the same twenty-four hours in a day? It is because these people produce much higher

---

[5] https://www.businessinsider.in/Heres-How-Much-10-Of-The-Richest-People-In-The-World-Made-Per-Minute-In-2013/articleshow/27660303.cms

value per hour than you and I do. Therefore, it proves that there is a non-linear relationship between the time invested and the value created out of such time.

The ultra-successful people have done this with the power of high-leverage thinking. What does this high-leverage thinking do? It works wonder because it sharpens the decision-making abilities of the individual. Such individuals with high-leverage thinking abilities are able to make decisions at a very fast pace.

In *Think and Grow Rich*, Napoleon Hill states the distinction between successful people and not so successful people. He explains that successful people have the capability to make any decisions at a faster pace. These people are very fast in making decisions in any field of life, but they are slow in reversing any decision or going back from what they had decided already. But if you look at average people, they take a long time in deciding something in the first place and ironically have the tendency to quickly change that decision or return to the previous position.

I heard one interview and was amazed to know that Richard Branson, the founder of Virgin Atlantic, knows within a matter of sixty seconds of meeting any new person whether he should do business with that person or not. Similarly, Warren Buffett is known to make his heavy-sized investment decisions quicker.

So now the question comes how do they develop this high-leverage thinking that helps to sharpen their decision-making abilities. There are few essential habits or frameworks in which these people operate their life. Let's look at the essential elements that trigger high-leverage thinking.

i. Reading Obsessively

One of the main habits of successful people is that they read a lot. Reading is feeding your mind with the wisdom of people who have researched into such topics and poured the knowledge in the form of filtered wisdom in the form of books. In my other books also, I have time and again repeated the significance of reading books. I will briefly state few examples of the reading habits of highly successful people:

Warren Buffett had a habit of reading 600 to 1000 pages every day when he was starting out his investing career. Even today, 80% of his working time is reading. Once he was asked about the keys to his success, he immediately pointed towards a stack of books nearby and said, *"Read 500 pages like this every day. That's how knowledge works. It builds up, like compound interest. All of you can do it, but I guarantee not many of you will do it."*

Similarly, Bill Gates is known to read 50 books a year; that is roughly one book a week. Mark Cuban reads more 3 hours every day. Elon Musk was once asked how he learned to build rockets and he admitted that he read books.

These people are highly selective in their readings and don't just read anything, because the objective of their reading is to get educated and not simply being entertained.

The next point will explain the specific types of readings of these individuals and how it helps them in high-leverage thinking.

ii. Study Things That Don't Change

The ultra-successful people primarily study the things that don't change. In other words, they focus more on the principles or theories that operate over a longer-term horizon instead of spending time on short-term tactics or tricks. They don't spend more time on things like how to increase your conversion ratio on the email opt-in at your website. Rather, they study the different disciplines of knowledge. They learn psychology and philosophy with equal passion as they study physics, mathematics, accounting, and any other discipline of knowledge. Once they have studied multiple streams of knowledge, their mind does the job of fusing the knowledge taken from different disciplines and then the power of synthesis comes into play.

As we all know, our mind is a complex super computer. With tons of information fed into their minds, the minds of these ultra-achievers start to synthesise the information by firing up neurons and forming multiple neuron connections. The forming of neuron connections means that the information absorbed from different disciplines of study fuse with each other and then they are able to make conclusion much better and much faster as compared to the normal human beings.

Justine Musk's (Elon Musk's ex-wife) statement below aptly describes the power of synthesis of the knowledge or information taken from different streams. She states:

"Choose one thing and become a master of it. Choose a second thing and become a master of that. When you become a master of two worlds (say, engineering and business), you can bring them together in a way that will a) introduce hot ideas to each other, so they can have idea sex and make idea babies that no one has seen before and b) create a competitive advantage because you can move between worlds, speak both languages, connect the tribes, mash the elements to spark fresh creative insight until you wake up with the epiphany that changes your life."

iii. The Power of Mental Models

Charlie Munger, the business partner of Warren Buffett, also a billionaire and considered Warren Buffett's right hand, of was fond of building mental models for effective decision-making.

A mental model is an approach of mentally filing away a massive, but finite amount of fundamental, unchanging knowledge to form the tools that can be used in evaluating the infinite number of unique scenarios arising in the real world.

In a famous speech in the 1990s, Munger explained his approach to gaining practical wisdom:

"Well, the first rule is that you can't really know anything if you just remember isolated facts and try and bang 'em back. If the facts don't hang together on a latticework of theory, you don't have them in a usable form.

You've got to have models in your head. And you've got to array your experience both vicarious and direct on this latticework of models. You may have noticed students who just try to remember and pound back what is remembered. Well, they fail in school and in life. You've got to hang experience on a latticework of models in your head.

What are the models? Well, the first rule is that you've got to have multiple models because if you just have one or two that you're using, the nature of human psychology is such that you'll torture reality so that it fits your models, or at least you'll think it does. ...

And the models have to come from multiple disciplines because all the wisdom of the world is not to be found in one little academic department. That's why poetry professors, by and large, are so unwise in a worldly sense. They don't have enough models in their heads. So you've got to have models across a fair array of disciplines.

You may say, "My God, this is already getting way too tough." But, fortunately, it isn't that tough because 80 or 90 important models will carry about 90% of the freight in making you a worldly wise person. And, of those, only a mere handful really carry very heavy freight."

Munger's system is like "cross-training for the mind." Instead of compartmentalizing ourselves in the small, limited areas we may have studied in school, we study a broadly useful set of knowledge about the world, which will serve us in all parts of life.

Therefore, you would realize that learning the mental models formed on the basis of different disciplines of study that will help you make better decisions based on established principles of nature already working in the background to operate the world. Once you acquire knowledge from most of the disciplines and synthesise it in your mind, you have attained worldly wisdom.

Here's a great description of the concept of worldly wisdom from Robert Griffin's book *Charlie Munger: The Complete Investor*

"Munger has adopted an approach to business and life that he refers to as worldly wisdom. Munger believes that by using a range of different models from many different disciplines—psychology, history, mathematics, physics, philosophy, biology, and so on—a person can use the combined output of the synthesis to produce something that has more value than the sum of its parts. ....each discipline entwines with, and in the process, strengthens every other. From each discipline the thoughtful person draws significant mental models, the key ideas that combine to produce a cohesive understanding. Those who cultivate this broad view are well on their way to achieving worldly wisdom."

Therefore, one who spends time in learning these mental models from different disciplines of life has a definite edge over most of the other population, who are just focussing in limited disciplines of knowledge. This edge of world wisdom helps them in to steeply improve their decision-making ability. Investing your time in learning the mental model is the best investment one can have to strongly leverage his thinking and thus generate more value from his time.

2. Determine Your Performance Necessity

Most people complain that despite setting goals, making plans, and then working towards their goals, and despite having good intentions, often they don't achieve success sooner or keep missing their goals by small margins.

Why is this so?

Welcome to the concept of Performance Necessity. It means you generally don't put your best shot forward until you see your performance becoming absolutely necessary. Most of the time, you feel like you are working towards your goals, but in reality, there is still something lacking due to which you are in that high state of emotion, necessary to achieve a particular goal. But few people will make their best performance a necessity in their mind. When you make something a necessity, then you are totally in a different frame of mind; you are willing to put in everything you have to just perform at your best and achieve your goal.

I heard one of Brendon Burchard's interviews and just had a feeling of 'awe' or a deep inspiration when I learned about few examples of what forms a performance necessity. Brendon Burchard is the best-selling author of multiple books, and an online trainer, having trained more than 2 million people online through his courses or books. These examples will help you understand what is meant by performance necessity and how it operates an individual to play his best game.

Have you ever thought about what ticks a sprinter to win a race, as compared to other participants in the race? As, you know, the difference between the winner and the first runner up is merely a fraction of a second, so no doubt one has to be at the top of his mental and physical game. But there is something else deep inside us that needs to be triggered to make a difference in such a scenario – and that deep emotion generates the performance necessity. Brendon shares that once he asked a high- achiever sprinter about how'd a sprinter know who'd win the race? The response of the athlete was touching – he stated that the sprinter who immediately before the start of the race looks at the audience and determines that he'd need to win the race for his mother or someone close to him has already generated a performance necessity;

therefore, all other things being equal, this sprinter creates an edge over the other participants in the race and thus significantly increases the chance of his success. The reason being that the moment one shifts the core reason for his success to someone outside of him, whom he loves or wants to see happy, the emotions in the body change the quality of your action to an altogether different level. His internal state of mind considers his performance to be an utmost necessity.

Brendon shared in the interview one of his personal incident that turned out to be his performance necessity and led him to earn 4.6 million US dollars in a short period of eighteen months. His performance necessity moment is really a heart touching one.

Brendon narrates about his past that he had been going through a difficult phase of life, where after having quitted the corporate job he was striving to establish himself as an author and as an online personal development trainer. One night, he was sitting writing in his one-bedroom apartment on the bed and his bills for expenses, other documents, etc. were lying on his quilt over the bed. He was casually writing and then noted that his girlfriend entered the room slowly. She didn't want to disturb Brendon in his writing, so she came slowly and crawled herself silently under the quilt. The same quilt – that was piled up with Brendon's expense invoices and other documents. As she went inside the quilt for sleeping, Brendon felt a really squeaking emotion in his heart. He said to himself, *"Oh My God, my lady is lying under the burden of my bills. How can I let that continue"?* Brendon further states that it was a moment of epiphany for him and he wrote much more and much better at that night. From that moment onwards, he didn't stop and then within a period of eighteen months, he earned 4.6 million US dollars as a best-selling author and one of the most sought out high-performance trainers in the world.

You can see the power of performance necessity. Therefore, you need to look around and determine what your performance necessity is? Do you see your young kids as factors to make your performance a necessity? Is your mother or father or your beloved or spouse someone who triggers your performance necessity? Once you fill your heart with the emotions towards that person, you will see a drastic surge in your productivity. Suddenly all the excuses or obstacles that seemed large earlier start appearing small in front of your performance necessity.

> ***"Rational thoughts never drive people's creativity the way emotions do." ~ Neil deGrasse Tyson***

3. Reprogram Your Mind by RWID Framework

As you already know, maintaining the right state on a consistent basis is the most important element out of all 3Ss of Success. The other two tools, i.e., Story and Strategy, don't work if we fail to control our state of mind.

You will learn in this section how you can control your state of mind to operate at the most resourceful levels possible most of the time so you can take massive inspired action. Before we get deeper into it, let's revisit how our minds operate.

Our minds are continuously being exposed on a regular basis to the outside environment. Of course, someone is not sitting in front of you always and is intentionally programming your mind to operate in a particularly negative way (there could be exceptions, however, when few people are specifically trained to believe in a certain way – like in armed forces or say training for terrorism). But if we remain in the same environment for a longer period, our mind starts to form a particular belief system based on these outside stimulants.

Further, our mind wants to optimize our living and that too without making much effort. Therefore, the easiest thing in front of mind is to operate based on the things that have happened in our past. For example, if your parents and most of your relatives had jobs in their lives, there are strong chances that you will start your career with a job. It happens because you start believing it is the right approach. You might think it is your own belief, but in reality, this belief had been deeply engrained in you through your continuous staying and observing a particular environment for a long period.

Our beliefs are formed based on repetitive thinking in a particular way. The definition of belief itself is the repetition of the same thoughts over and over for a long period of time. In the formation of beliefs or programming of the mind, the RWID framework plays a vital role. I heard the concept from Brendon Burchard in one of his resources.

RWID stands for **R**elative **W**eight of **I**mportance and **D**uration

This framework operates on the premise that certain thoughts program our minds, if we give relatively more weight to some thoughts as important ones and if we allow that thought to retain in our mind for a long period.

Let me explain by way of an example through portraying two different thought scenarios to show how RWID framework operates.

Suppose I want to speak at a TED Talk Show (One of the best platforms in the world for thought leaders for expressing their opinions) as one of the key accomplishments of my life. Anyone would say it is really a big task to accomplish. Now, initial thoughts that might come to my mind would be:

- I am not good at speaking or maybe I don't have a strong vocabulary or command over the language.
- I don't have knowledge of the subject or the uniqueness that I can eloquently explain my perspective on the topic for twenty minutes.
- I feel like sweating and trembling at the mere thought of standing on a TED stage.
- I also don't have a good-looking face, so maybe people will laugh at me.
- And maybe some other negative thoughts.

Now see the RWID framework in operation here. If I am consistently thinking the above thoughts, it means I am spending a longer duration on these thoughts and also since I am regularly thinking, I am giving importance to these thoughts. Hence, I have given relatively higher weight in terms of importance and duration to these negative thoughts. With this approach, it is not possible to even take the first step, because I have formed and further strengthened a belief by programming my mind that I won't be able to do that.

Now take another thought scenario, which is a much better approach to thinking different thoughts. New thoughts could be as follows:

- What is so special about those people who have spoken on the TED Talks? Maybe I can also learn this.
- What are the subject knowledge and skill sets these people possess that I need to acquire to deliver a talk?
- If they can do it, probably I can also do it with necessary preparation.
- It may be difficult; it may require learning newer things; it may be

time consuming – but it may not be an impossible thing to achieve.
- I am sure I have something unique about myself that can add value to the lives of people around me; it just requires packaging and presentation before the audience.

If I continuously now choose these second thought scenarios over the negative thoughts in the first scenario, the principle of RWID can work in my favour. With such thoughts, I may be inclined to watch the people giving TED Talks closely. I might start following them on their blogs or social media to know more about how they had been able to achieve that goal. The principles of RWID can change my program and help me think differently, so my actions will be different.

Of course, there will be a challenge in overcoming the first scenario, because it is not only you who thinks that way; rather, the people around you further reinforce your negative thinking and therefore it becomes a herculean task to shift our thinking towards possibility. Therefore, it requires consistent observation of our thoughts and switching from negative thoughts to resourceful thoughts moment to moment.

Since now you know it well that principle of RWID works to re-program your mind by giving importance and time to certain thoughts. So instead of the thoughts automatically running through your mind, you need to give your mind a choice to run specific thoughts. I know it will seem like bit philosophical and your mind will oppose you or ridicule you for choosing highly ambitious thoughts. It is because it would not seem logical to your mind in the first place, as it doesn't have any past experience to support that new thought. But here is the thing. You need to understand and deeply convince your mind that if negative thoughts through repetition and importance have become your beliefs, the same principle can be applied to create positive beliefs in your life. It will take initial time and some struggle with your own mind, but it is worth investing time doing RWID for imbibing resourceful and ambitious thoughts.

With that understanding, it is only a matter of what thoughts you allow to run in your head. Whether you believe it or not, as humans, we have been given the consciousness to take decisions and make choices. But at the cost of repetition, I would emphasise that the root of the problem is that most people don't exercise the choice of thinking resourceful thoughts to achieve their goals.

For example, you have a choice to watch a Netflix thriller and drama series or watch an online knowledge development course. Don't you think you have a choice here? Yes, you have. But we don't exercise that choice wisely towards a better life.

The RWID framework is a philosophy or a principle on which our mind operates. This is the operating manual, of course simple, but not an easy one to implement. Because it requires moment-to-moment work in choosing to allow the right set of thoughts to enter your mind. The more weight you start giving to your positive thoughts, the more you will be able to positively rewire your mind. I believe that if one can maintain such positive thoughts for just thirty days, it has the power to rewire your brain and reprogram your mindset. Once you start doing it and do enough of it, the magic will start happening.

Because if you think you can do it, you will generate resourceful emotions and feel better about doing it. With better emotions, you will take the necessary action towards your goals and that action will show you results. Even a small amount of progress will improve your confidence. That improved confidence will help you to think more about the positive thoughts that, in turn, will generate further action.

So this consistent loop of positive thoughts, then followed by positive actions and behaviour will multiply the effect of RWID principle, and soon you will realize that you have an altogether different thinking pattern. You will realize that you remain in the positive state more often. This positive state will help you create new positive stories. With that, you will increase your resourcefulness.

Tony Robbins repeatedly says that you don't suffer due to lack of resources; you suffer due to lack of resourcefulness. The resourcefulness will present more strategies in front of you to take action and the day will not be far when you will start attaining your goals and dreams without suffering an internal struggle.

I hope you will try out this simple technique with a dose of discipline for at least the next thirty days to see the results on your own.

4. Clarity Seeking Is Never Ending & How to Clear Your Thinking

Someone might ask if one is already successful and clear about where he is going, what further clarity is required at this stage? You might think only someone who is not able to make both ends meet would require clarity about the direction to follow in life.

But this is not the case. Everyone needs a regular dose of clarity on a consistent basis, at whatever stage of life he or she is in. There is a reason behind that. Our life daily unfolds before us and presents a variety of circumstances that are entirely new and never faced by us in the past – and no one is equipped with all the solutions in advance to handle all the situations of life. Therefore, there is a need to seek clarity on the approach to be followed or action to be taken while facing the new events in one's life.

Another reason is that as humans we are thinking creatures, as well as a social animal – we are either with ourselves or with someone outside, thus either moulded by our own thoughts or influenced by the outside environment we interact on a regular basis.

Our mind consistently keeps on generating one thought or the other every time of our waking life. Also, most of us go out of our homes to earn our living and therefore connect with people on a regular basis – this also exposes our mind to different thoughts. Besides the above, we are connected to a large number of social media platforms on more than a regular basis. Whatever time is left after all this is spent on media, news, television, the internet, etc, which keeps us consistently engaged. For example, if the media is spreading the news that the economy is going downside or that a change in the ruling party will have an adverse impact on your business or job or any other kind of negative thoughts, this impacts your thinking process.

All this summed up has a much greater influence on your mind and clarity of your thinking process than you can imagine. And the obvious outcome of all this bombarding leads to cluttering or suppressing your inner voice and hampers clear thinking.

Everyone faces this situation. Most people depend more on outside approval and thus encounter this situation quite often. This adversely affects the quality of their decisions, as their heads are clouded with contrasting thoughts. If one remains in such a situation and doesn't take any steps to correct the situation, such person would not be in a position to take best decisions, due to lack of clarity.

Therefore, the people who have reached the top have made a daily habit to invest some time in gaining clarity on their next step in their life.

How do they enhance their inner clarity?

Thankfully, Tim Ferriss, best-selling author of many books, has explored the answer for us. Tim has interviewed on his podcast show more than two hundred high achievers, including billionaires, sportsmen, and celebrities like Arnold Schwarzenegger, Jamie Foxx, Edward Norton, Tony Robbins, Maria Sharapova, Peter Thiel, Amanda Palmer, and Malcolm Gladwell to name a few. Based on his interaction with the ultra-performers and high achievers, he states that more than 90% of the people he interviewed have instilled a habit of going inside their mind and bodies to observe their mind and the thoughts, emotions, and sensation going on in their body. They have adopted mindfulness or some other form of meditation practice in their daily routine. Below quote aptly justifies why these high achievers do so.

> *"The power within us is infinite. Plug into your higher self for a surge that will propel you to places you thought unattainable."*
> *~Mary-Frances Winters*

Steve Jobs is famous for his great ability to create innovative and groundbreaking products. But not everyone knows that Steve Jobs was a pioneer in the use of Zen mindfulness meditation to reduce his stress, gain more clarity, and enhance his creativity. Biographer Walter Isaacson quotes Jobs as saying[6]:

---

[6] https://www.inc.com/geoffrey-james/how-steve-jobs-trained-his-own-brain.html

"If you just sit and observe, you will see how restless your mind is. If you try to calm it, it only makes it worse, but over time it does calm, and when it does, there's room to hear more subtle things – that's when your intuition starts to blossom and you start to see things more clearly and be in the present more. Your mind just slows down, and you see a tremendous expanse in the moment. You see so much more than you could see before."

That's the power of mindfulness to calm your mind and enable you to think clearly and enhance your intuition to attract solutions to your life problems.

Mindfulness can simply be defined as a practice of maintaining a non-judgmental state of heightened or complete awareness of one's thoughts, emotions, or experiences on a moment-to-moment basis.

Those who believe the myth that mindfulness is only for spiritual or religious reasons or find this a philosophical approach would be surprised to know neuroscience has proved that mindfulness helps to improve your cognitive abilities significantly. There are now enough neuroscience experiments and research that show an increase in physical size of brain portions like hippocampus (responsible for memory), pre-frontal cortex (for memory and executive decision making). It also has shown the reduction in the size of brain structure like amygdala (that is responsible for fear and also generates a reaction of flight or fight). Mindfulness has shown to reduce the stress, improve focus, improves emotional intelligence, and has shown that it has the impact of slowing down the ageing of our brains.

Today mindfulness has become a part of the mainstream in the modern high-tech environment. Companies like Google and Facebook have started conducting mindfulness sessions at their office. This has also spread to the government office and even at parliament in many countries like the US, UK, Sweden etc. Schools, prisons, and even law firms are also using this.

Now how does it help to attain better clarity?

The mindfulness practice trains you to disengage yourself and thus observe your thoughts and emotions as different from yourself. You don't associate yourself with your thoughts, rather you become capable to stand aside and observe all your thoughts, emotions and sensations going on inside your body. This enhanced observation capacity helps you to see the distinction between different ongoing thoughts and make your decisions objectively instead of getting confused signals, which is the property of a wandering mind.

How can you incorporate mindfulness into your life?

It doesn't demand any specific setup or instrument to incorporate mindfulness into your daily routine. Rather, it is simply a matter of putting yourself to discipline for a dedicated amount of time per day. You may start this for ten minutes a day by setting your timer for ten minutes. You don't need to sit on the ground in a half-lotus position; rather, you can sit comfortably on any chair – just ensure that spine is straight and not bent. You need to then start watching your breath going in with each inhale and going out with each exhale. When breath enters your body, you need to track and feel all the places of your body where it touches, i.e., your nostrils, your throat, chest and then finally your abdomen. A similar process you need to observe when you are exhaling your breath, e.g., notice the sensation of breath on all your inner parts. During this process of observation of your breath, notice all the thoughts in your mind and emotions arising in your body.

Also, one key point, you don't need to feel guilty if while sitting in meditation sometimes you realize that you had lost your attention on your breath, thoughts, or emotions. The moment you realize that you lost your attention, you simply need to get your attention get back. In fact, if you are able to realize that you had digressed, that in itself is a sign of gaining mindfulness.

For those who have never tried meditation or sitting idle for a few minutes, you may gain support from many mobile apps on mindfulness. These apps give you guided instructions, which will enable you to gain all the advantages of practicing mindfulness.

You can explore a few mobile apps, namely, Headspace, Welzen, or Calm, and start your mindfulness practice with either of them.

Whatever suits your needs better, you can always get further into that practice.

If you are interested to know about mindfulness in detail, i.e., about its origin, meditational, and practical aspects, the scientific studies, and how you can start immediately incorporate mindfulness into your life, you may want to check out my book *The Mindful Mind*, which I am sure will be beneficial to you.

5. Catapult Your Self-Image through Mental Training

Studies now show that the athletes who practice more mentally than those who practice physically have shown better results. In one study, experiments were conducted on the training methods of four groups of athletes as shown below:

- Group one: 100% physical training
- Group two: 75% physical training, 25% mental training

- Group three: 50% physical training, 50% mental training
- Group four: 25% physical training, 75% mental training

The fourth group had the best results overall, outperforming the competition in the Olympics.

Lanny Bassham, an American sports shooter, who was an Olympics gold medallist, has written his bestseller book titled *With Winning at Mind,* in which he described how the top five percent athletes of the world play their game. Lanny claims to have spoken to hundreds of Olympic athletes and PGA tour pros about their secrets of high performance. And every one of them had answered unequivocally that at least 90% of their game was a mental game.

Bassham explains that the whole mental game is a complex one and needs enough practice to master this. The mental game comprises three necessary elements as listed below:

a. Your conscious mind
b. Your subconscious mind
c. Your self-image.

We all know our conscious mind is just a tip of the iceberg. It is even less than 5% of your mind and works primarily on one thing at a time, thus focusing on the work at hand only. But beneath this layer of conscious mind there lies our subconscious mind that keeps on working hundred percent of the time, even when we are sleeping. We don't ever have to worry about pumping the blood to our entire body, taking a breath or digesting food, or any other body function; this all happens on an autopilot basis through our subconscious mind.

But the most important point to note here is that not only these almost autonomous bodily functions, but the majority of our decisions are carried out depending upon the programming of our mind from our childhood since the time we start to understand from our environment. You might think you are deciding on your day-to-day problem using your conscious mind, but in reality, most of your decisions are taken based on your belief system through consistent impressions on your subconscious mind from your environment.

For example, if you are born with a family where everyone has a job. Then for your entire childhood and teenage years, you will continue to listen to the voices like, "You have to study hard, get good grades, and get a well-paying job." So when you are in high school or are finishing your graduation, all these thoughts are very well programmed in your subconscious mind and belief system. Now if you see some of your friends venturing into a new business system, but you simply stick to finding the best job for you; then don't assume that it is your own chosen decision to go for that job. Rather, these beliefs are so deeply imbibed in your subconscious mind that you believe it is your own decision.

Just to test it differently, assume for a moment a different scenario. Assume that you are born and brought up in a wealthy business family. In this case, there is a high probability that you would think about setting up your own business. There is a low probability that you would think about searching for a job, despite the fact that you have scored good grades in your studies. Again, your decision is based on your subconscious mind.

Now let's talk about the third element – your self-image. Based on your subconscious mind, which is highly influenced by your environment, your beliefs are formed and you start seeing yourself as a specific type of person. That determines your performance in any area of your life.

Finally, this entire mental game with the above three elements works like this:

a. Our Conscious mind focuses on our thoughts.
b. Our Subconscious mind is responsible for our physical performance.
c. Our Self-image ultimately drives our performance.

Lanny explains that your self-image "makes you perform like you." It keeps you within your comfort zone. If you are below your zone, self-image makes you uncomfortable and turns up your power until you are within the zone. Likewise, if you are above your zone, the self-image will reduce your energy and power, dropping you back within your zone.

As long as you "perform like you," the self-image does not interfere. Therefore, to change your performance, you must change your self-image and elevate your comfort zone. Controlling that change in your self-image may be the most important skill you will ever learn. You can change any attitude you do not like. The crux is that when the self-image changes, performance changes.

How do you change your self-image?

Fortunately, there is a simple way to change your self-image. You can do it through what is called "Imprinting."

Whatever image you have of yourself now has formed by years of imprinting on your mind through your surrounding environment. If you want to create a fresh and desired self-image, it requires another form of imprinting. Instead of allowing the imprinting to happen through your environment, you have to consciously choose the kind of imprinting you want to have on your mind.

Let's consider reshaping your mind to changing your physical body. If you wish to achieve a goal of fat loss or gain muscle, you need to follow a specific regime or exercise and diets. You can't just eat anything and can't ignore your exercise program. The same is the case with mental reshaping. You can't allow any kind of thought to enter your mind and you would not simply stay in your comfort zone and expect the changes on its own. You have to consciously choose your thoughts, consistently expose your mind to a newer way of thinking, and by regular exposure to the new environment, you will start believing differently about yourself and look yourself differently. That way you will internalize a new self-image of yourself.

With a new self-image of yourself, you think of yourself as a different person, as a person who can achieve the goals you imagine. And this is the game changer, as there is no internal conflict – you have embraced a new image and therefore you will now act as per your new self-image and can achieve your goals faster.

6. How to Use Visualization To Design Your Future

> *"Visualization is the human being's vehicle to the future – good, bad or indifferent. It's strictly in our control"* ~ Earl Nightingale

There is no better way to explain this concept than through a real-life example. In his book, *The Success Principles: How to Get From Where You Are to Where You Want to Be*, Jack Canfield narrates a story explaining the massive power of visualization by American Gymnast and Olympic Gold Medallist Peter Vidmar in his pursuit of winning gold. The story is vividly explained by Vidmar in his own words in Jack's book, and you will be amazed to see the power of visualization to achieve massive goals so smoothly. Here is the relevant story excerpt as narrated in the words of Vidmar:

> To keep us focused on our Olympic goal, we began ending our workouts by visualizing our dream. We visualized ourselves actually competing in the Olympics and achieving our dream by practicing what we thought would be the ultimate gymnastics scenario.
>
> I'd say, "Okay, Tim, let's imagine it's the men's gymnastics team finals of the Olympic Games.
>
> The United States team is on its last event of the night, which just happens to be the high bar. The last two guys up for the United States are Tim Daggett and Peter Vidmar. Our team is neck and neck with the People's Republic of China, the reigning world champions, and we have to perform our routines

perfectly to win the Olympic team gold medal.

At that point, we'd each be thinking, *Yeah, right. We're never going to be neck and neck with those guys. They were number one at the Budapest world championships, while our team didn't even win a medal. It's never going to happen.*

But what if it did happen? How would we feel?

We'd close our eyes and, in this empty gym at the end of a long day, we'd visualize an Olympic arena with 13,000 people in the seats and another 200 million watching live on television. Then we'd practice our routines. First, I'd be the announcer. I'd cup my hands around my mouth and say, "Next up, from the United States of

America, Tim Daggett." Then Tim would go through his routine as if it were the real thing.

Then Tim would go over to the corner of the gym, cup his hands around his mouth, and, in his best announcer voice, say, "Next up, from the United States of America, Peter Vidmar." Then it was my turn. In my mind, I had one chance to perfectly perform my routine in order for our team to win the gold medal. If I didn't, we'd lose.

Tim would shout out, "Green light," and I'd look at the superior judge, who was usually our coach Mako. I'd raise my hand, and he'd raise his right back. Then I'd turn, face the bar, grab hold, and begin my routine.

Well, a funny thing happened on July 31, 1984.

It was the Olympic Games, men's gymnastics team finals in Pauley Pavilion on the UCLA campus. The 13,000 seats were all filled, and a television audience in excess of 200 million around the world tuned in. The United States team was on its last event of the night, the high bar. The last two guys up for the United States just happened to be Tim Daggett and Peter Vidmar. And just as we visualized, our team was neck and neck with the People's Republic of China. We had to perform our high bar routines perfectly to win the gold medal.

I looked at Coach Mako, my coach for the past 12 years. As focused as ever, he simply said, "Okay, Peter, let's go. You know what to do. You've done it a thousand times, just like every day back in the gym.

Let's just do it one more time and let's go home. You're prepared."

He was right. I had planned for this moment and visualized it hundreds of times. I was prepared to perform my routine. Rather than seeing myself actually standing in the Olympic arena with 13,000 people in the stands and 200 million watching on television, in my mind I pictured myself back in the UCLA gym at the end of the day with two people left in the gym.

When the announcer said, "From the United States of America, Peter Vidmar," I imagined it was my buddy Tim Daggett saying it. When the green light came on, indicating it was time for the routine, I imagined that it wasn't really a green light but that it was Tim shouting, "Green light!" And when I raised my hand toward the superior judge from East Germany, in my mind I was signalling my coach, just like I had signalled him every day at the end of hundreds of workouts. In the gym, I always visualized I was at the Olympic finals. At the Olympic finals, I visualized I was back in the gym.

I turned, faced the bar, jumped up, and grabbed on. I began the same routine I had visualized and practiced day after day in the gym. I was in memory mode, going yet again where I'd already gone hundreds of times. I quickly made it past the risky double-release move that had harpooned my chances at the world championships. I moved smoothly through the rest of my routine and landed a solid dismount, where I anxiously waited for my score from the judges.

With a deep voice, the announcement came through the speaker, "The score for Peter Vidmar is 9.95." "Yes!" I shouted. "I did it!" The crowd cheered loudly as my teammates and I celebrated our victory.

Thirty minutes later, we were standing on the Olympic medal platform in the Olympic arena with 13,000 people in the stands and over 200 million watching on television, while the gold medals were officially draped around our necks. Tim, me, and our teammates stood proudly wearing our gold medals as the national anthem played and the American flag was raised to the top of the arena. It was a moment we visualized and practiced hundreds of times in the gym. Only this time, it was for real.

What an amazing real-life story! It explains the immense power of visualization to achieve your dreams. Now depending on whatever your dreams or goals are, you can start visualizing achieving your dreams by putting in the requisite actions.

The above story demonstrates that visualization is the process of sharpening your mental game, which supports in your outward endeavours in order to achieve your goals. In this process, you visualize your dreams as if you have already achieved them and imagine living your desired life. The visualisation process involves seeing the vivid images clearly. It is very helpful if you use all your senses in the process of visualization. Lisa Nichols, in her guided visualization techniques, helps you visualize your ideal future as follows:

For example, if your goal is to live in your dream house. You have to vividly imagine your dream house to the finest of the details. You need to smell the lavender or sandal fragrance or whatever is your favourite one in the different rooms of your house. You might visualize a crystal chandelier hanging in your living room. You will see a fully furnished kitchen with all the amenities therein. Visit your master bedroom with vibrant colours over there. Look at your children's room with beautiful colours and all modern toys. Now just imagine that you are staying happily in that house with your family member. Go to the extent of imagining that your family members are appreciating you for all your success achieved. Hear their sound what you would actually hear. Hear your spouse or better half saying, "I am proud of you. I am deeply inspired by you. You have shown me the height of human potential by your consistent efforts towards your goals." Hear all these sounds as if all of this is true and happening in reality.

The most important point is to let your emotions flow as openly as possible. If you feel your chest filling with deep emotions let it overflow. It may happen that your eyes are filled with tears. Let that happen. Because:

> *"Whatever we plant in our subconscious mind and nourish with repetition and emotion will one day become a reality."* ~ *Earl Nightingale*

You would agree that there is no better to test the human potential other than sports. Most of the sports coaches strongly advocate the importance of visualization before the real success ever comes to you, as you noted from the Olympics Gold Medal story above. But why is it so?

It is because our subconscious mind doesn't understand the difference between reality and the imagination. It only starts thinking something as true whatever is thought more often by an individual. Further our subconscious mind is more influenced by the images than the words. If you continuously visualize the objects of your dreams in the form of images and add the power of emotions, then it influences your subconscious mind at a deeper level.

By regular practices of say 4–6 weeks of this visualization process, your subconscious mind starts to rewire. Now when it sees a conflict between the images in the subconscious mind and the reality scenario of your life, it starts to throw open the ideas that will help you to move towards your dreams.

When you are doing the job of rewiring your subconscious mind, then you have to work like a gardener. A gardener knows very well that one doesn't need to take any active steps for weeds to grow in the garden. Weeds don't require any specific water treatment, fertilizer, specific type of land, or any other special arrangement;

they simply appear on their own between the cracks. The same is the case with negative thinking; it also comes on its own. You don't have to take any specific steps to let the negative thinking come to you. Rather, if you let your mind loose, only negative thinking will come to you, as our minds are biased towards thinking negatively.

But now as a gardener, if you have to grow up orchids or any other kinds of flowers in your garden, you know it requires a specific protocol to follow. You need a specific type of fertile land, the perfect quality of seeds – you need the right exposure of sunlight and the watering of these plants. Besides all of the above, you need to take care of your flowers by protecting them from being infected by any bug or virus. After doing all that steps for a longer time, then only you can see the fruits of your labour. After all these precautions only, a gardener is able to see the vibrantly colourful flowers.

Therefore, to get a pull effect working in your life – a pull by some unseen force towards your dream, you need to act like a gardener. While on the one hand, you have to put efforts by planting the positive thoughts through visualizing and then running these positive thoughts in your mind the whole day; on the other hand, you need to ensure that you need to stay protected from people or circumstances which create the negative thoughts in your minds.

If you continuously visualize yourself doing certain specific things and achieving specific results, your subconscious mind will connect with the infinite intelligence to bring certain specific events or people to your life. This will help you take an inspired action towards your dreams.

Harness the power of the Reticular Activating System through visualization

Visualization affects the operations of the reticular activating system in your brain. The Reticular Activating System (RAS) is a bundle of nerves at our brainstem that filters out unnecessary information so the important stuff gets through. The RAS is the reason you learn a new word and then start hearing it everywhere. It's why you can tune out a crowd full of talking people, yet immediately snap to attention when someone says your name or something that at least sounds like it.

Let's me try to explain it further. Our brains are consistently bombarded with million bytes of information every minute. It is not possible for our mind to let all the data and information in; hence it deploys a filtering system. This system allows only that type of information that your mind finds relevant and mostly thinking about.

If you are consistently thinking about the downfall of the economy, stressed financial market or say losing your job, your mind will filter all other information and look only for such things which match with your dominant thought process. Now once you start visualization, the dominant thoughts in your head are only about your dreams. With that, your mind now starts filtering the information that makes you reach closer to your dreams. Now RAS works to your benefit, which earlier was working to your detriment.

Visualization – a different approach – mental contrasting

Heidi Grant Halvorson, in her best-selling book, *Succeed,* talks about a slightly different approach to visualization. She specifically recommends the specific strategy of mental contrasting. In this approach, first you imagine attaining your goal, and then you reflect on the obstacles that stand in the way. If you want to get a high-paying job, start by imagining yourself accepting an offer at a top firm, and then think about what stands between you and that offer—there are many other equally qualified candidates there, you need to figure out why would you be selected? Also, you have to think if you have to apply for other available jobs if you don't succeed at one. That's called feeling the *necessity to act*—it's a psychological state crucial to achieving a goal.

She goes on to state further that merely dreaming (without any action plan) about how great it will feel to get your dream job or attain your financial goals, won't get you anywhere. Mental contrasting turns wishes and dreams into reality, by bringing into focus what you will need to do to make it happen.

7. Don't Rely on Willpower Solely

"Willpower is for people who are still uncertain about what they want to do."— Helia

The above quote might seem counter-intuitive to you.

It is because the whole world out there is advocating pretty loud that you must develop a strong willpower to take consistent action before you can achieve your goals. Everyone seems to suggest that you need to be a disciplined and sort of forcing yourself to take action.

But after personally experiencing it now, I am finding the above quote to be true. Let me try to explain it through a simple example why relying solely on willpower is not an effective approach. Assume you want to move a heavy object from one place to another. There are two ways to do it. The first approach is to apply all your force to move that object. But there is a second approach and the better one – where some power pulls that object and you have to apply a minimal amount of force or no force – you just have to support that pull to let the object move at its desired destination. Everyone would agree that pull effect is a more effective approach than entirely using your force.

The willpower approach is an approach of force. If you have to use your willpower to do something, it means that there is some resistance somewhere in your mind about performing that very activity.

For example, if you have to force yourself up in the morning to hit the gym or do any kind of physical activity – it means you are using your willpower to do that. Now assume you make a *decision* to participate in a half-marathon six months from now – note that it's not merely a wish, you have made a *decision*. You have not vaguely just thought about it. You are not thinking like, "If I could run, then it's fine – but if I somehow couldn't, then also it is fine." If that's the way you think, then you have not yet *truly decided* what you really want.

But the moment, you *decide* that you want to run that half-marathon, you will suddenly realize something pulling you towards it. On your own, you will be finding the running training blogs and videos. You will be taking care of your eating habits. If you had the habit of smoking or drinking or intoxicating yourself otherwise, this decision on its own will kill your desire to do anything that could halt your progress – as smoking curbs your ability to breathe deeper, which is mandatory for running longer.

Trust me, I have experimented with this in my personal life already. I decided a few years ago to participate in a short run and I had started preparing for that. Let me tell you, during that period, I stopped meeting my friends in the evening over the weekend – instead I met them on Sunday mornings at cafe restaurants. Why? Because meetings in the evening meant a few rounds of drinks with casual smoking – and my body's instant reaction was to avoid that. And I recall those days; I never felt I had to do a lot of sacrificing, rather it was my decision that kept me pulling towards it – I just felt like only supporting that decision. Therefore, my experience states that I didn't require any kind of willpower to do that thing.

> *"Once you make a decision, the universe conspires to make it happen."—Ralph Waldo Emerson*

You can experiment in relation to any of your actions whether you are using the force of willpower or your decision is pulling you towards it. Just think of some activity that is important for your progress. It could be preparing for your school or college project report, or your office presentation, or it could be any physical activity goal. Now if you have to struggle hard more often with your mind to start or stay put in that activity, it is a sign that you have not activated your real motivation behind the action. It means that your actions have not yet got the backing of the pull effect of your *decision*. In such a situation you would try to rely solely on your willpower.

I am not against exercising self-discipline or controlling your actions – these are virtues, but if you solely rely on willpower without making a true decision, your life will be more of a struggle rather than joy.

If you have got the power of pull by your decision, you will perform your actions almost effortlessly without any inner conflicts. If not, then you will often find yourself procrastinating or making excuses and then trying to compensate by exercising the force of willpower.

Forcing willpower is not a sustainable approach, as over a period of time, you will feel burned out and frustrated – the natural progression thereof will be finding excuses or delaying the work. Using the power of decisions will ignite your compelling reason, which empowers you with determination and persistence, and you will find yourself making progress on your life goals.

Tony Robbins once said:

"There are only two options: make progress or make excuses."

As the gravitation pull of earth makes everything comfortable staying and moving on the earth, in the same way, the pull of empowered decision keeps you sticking to your action without drifting often. Therefore, it is a much better and effective choice to get ourselves pulled by our decisions and not to force willpower to achieve our goals.

Napoleon Hill rightly quoted:

"When your desires are strong enough, you will appear to possess superhuman powers to achieve."

8. Ego Is the Enemy: How to Overcome It and Progress Faster

This might sound like some religious or spiritual preaching. But I am talking about it entirely from the perspective of success and the general well-being of a human being. Most of us even think we don't have an ego. You might think you are a decent person who is soft spoken and rarely speak in a loud voice or annoy someone. You might be a person who generally doesn't get angry easily, nor do you bully people in your home or office or in your community. If you do carry all these traits, you will obviously wonder, where does the question of ego come with such qualities?

Who can better tell than me? Because I personally feel I had been like that most of my life – the traits stated above fits me. But recently I have also realized that the most important requirement is to observe the inner conversation going on in our own heads, even if we are interacting with the outside world in the way stated above. Despite all these 'so called' pleasant personality traits, there are good chances that we might think something like the below:

- Why should I go to that person to learn something new, even if that fellow knows a lot on the subject? It is because I might have some false pride that I also carry knowledge on that aspect.
- That fellow is so much younger than me – what would he think of me if I approach him for guidance?
- I should avoid facing that person if he knows more than me, because otherwise my ignorance or lower level of knowledge will get exposed.

- Or maybe I have more money or resources than this person, so I should avoid meeting someone who has lesser resources but otherwise possesses knowledge or skills that can help me progress faster.

Now you can realize that on the one hand, your mind makes you put on a facade so that you yourself feel and also the outside world thinks you are a good person. Maybe that facade helps you to avoid any confrontation with the outside world, so this facade is helpful to that extent. But if inside your mind, thoughts like the above keep running, then it is your ego controlling your mind and thus affecting your behaviour and necessary action towards your goals.

Before we move ahead, let me clarify that ego is on a different extreme as compared to your self-esteem or self-respect. You must have a strong belief in yourself and your abilities. If someone tries to hurt you, oppose them and refuse to be bullied by anyone. But here we are talking about your inner emotion that stops you from approaching someone merely because you carry some false pride about your abilities – and this false facade is your ego. Here, ego does the job of constraining you to remain within yourself and ignore others, even if that person may be some help to you.

If you have an ego because you know a lot about the subject, then you would stop learning new things. You would hesitate to treat someone as a master to coach you doing new things.

That's why Ryan Holiday in his book *Ego Is the Enemy*, defines ego <u>as an unhealthy belief in our own importance</u>. He goes on to state,

"It's when the notion of ourselves and the world grows so inflated that it begins to distort the reality that surrounds us. When, as the football coach Bill Walsh explained, 'self-confidence becomes arrogance, assertiveness becomes obstinacy, and self-assurance becomes reckless abandon.' This is the ego, as the writer Cyril Connolly warned, that 'sucks us down like the law of gravity.'

In this way, ego is the enemy of what you want and of what you have: Of mastering your craft. Of real creative insight. Of working well with others. Of building loyalty and support. Of longevity. Of repeating and retaining your success. It repulses advantages and opportunities. It's a magnet for enemies and errors."

Yes, ego comes in the way of what is possible for you. Ego has the potential to halt your progress and can make you standstill in your own thought castle and you start thinking as if you have arrived. In a nutshell, ego will make you uncoachable. Ego will stop you from taking advantages from people around you, because you have closed your doors for anything new.

"Ego doesn't allow for proper incubation either. To become what we ultimately hope to become often takes long periods of obscurity, of sitting and wrestling with some topic or paradox. Humility is what keeps us there, concerned that we don't know enough and that we must continue to study. Ego rushes to the end, rationalizes that patience is for losers (wrongly seeing it as a weakness), and assumes we're good enough to give our talents a go in the

world." – Ryan Holiday

Just note that the journey of success never ends. At whatever level you reach, there is the next level to reach in your life. The top billionaires and highly successful people know this by heart. They know learning never ends and they are consistently ready to go anywhere to learn anything new.

Tony Robbins, who is one of the world's most influence strategist coach, himself says he doesn't mind flying to a different country and hire a coach to learn something new, even after achieving massive success already in his life. In his coaching experience, he states that people who are at the top of their business and careers are willing to spend money to get even a meagre one percent of an additional edge over the competitors, as that miniscule edge may help them earn millions of dollars in revenue and profits.

See despite reaching that stage, these people are still so humble to learn from others. And a normal man is plagued with the thinking that he knows a lot and doesn't need to learn any further.

Just think for a moment that for learning one discipline of education that helps us to secure an initial job of say fifty thousand dollars a year, we are ready to spend years in education. But when it comes to learning the life skills and learning the specific business or industry insights, we often close our minds, thinking we don't need anything further. It is nothing but ego sabotaging our progress.

Therefore, if you wish to be on the journey of consistent progress, don't let your ego get in your way. Be open. Be coachable.

> *"In a humble state, you learn better. I can't find anything else very exciting*

about humility, but at least there's that." ~ *John Dooner*

9. Redefine Failure: Fail Fast Forward To Success

This draws me to the last, but one of the most important factors to expedite your journey to success. It requires changing your definition of failure. It requires rewiring our belief system. It means we need to change our lenses of viewing this world differently and with an open approach.

Whenever we face the failure, we need to see that we are not failures; we're just experiencing failure. This single distinction in your mind will change the way you take action in the face of failure. The majority of us, in the face of failure, think of quitting; we think that if we are failing, then there must be something wrong with us. But those few who stay persistent and ultimately touch the apex of the mountain think differently. They consider failure as an experience.

We should treat failures like the experiments in the science laboratory. The scientists don't stop experimenting further if one experiment fails. For them, failure is just a data point. It simply shows that something didn't work yet fully.

In the words of Ellen Langer, *"**There are no failures, only ineffective solutions.**"*

It took Edison 9999 tries to invent the electric bulb, but that simply meant something was wrong with his approach that needed tweaking. Had he thought he was a failure in the initial few trials, he wouldn't have been able to give the gift of light to the world. In his own words:

"I haven't failed. I just found 10,000 ways that won't work."

Tal Ben-Shahar describes the importance of failure in his book, *The Pursuit of Perfect*, where he states: "One of the wishes that I always have for my students is that they should fail more often (although they are understandably not thrilled to hear me tell them so). If they fail frequently, it means that they try frequently, that they put themselves on the line and challenge themselves. It is only from the experience of challenging ourselves that we learn and grow, and we often develop and mature much more from our failures than from our successes. Moreover, when we put ourselves on the line, when we fall down and get up again, we become stronger and more resilient."

He further states that: "Those who understand that failure is inextricably linked with achievement are the ones who learn, grow, and ultimately do well. Learn to fail, or fail to learn."

In my other book, _Conquer Your Fear of Failure_, I have narrated the stories of the world's most famous and successful people, who have gone through dark times of failure and have come through it by persistence and continuous action. I have explained the ways to rewire your belief system to perceive fear differently and conquer your fear of failure. You may want to check out the book if you are sincerely looking for a solution to conquer your fear of failure.

Every great leader has talked favourably about failure, about embracing failure. Therefore, one should target failing fast but then moving further after failing. Once you have ascertained the definiteness of your purpose, take massive action on your goal. Why massive action? Because, once you take massive action, you will quickly start getting feedback from the world. You will notice which things are working and which are not. If you take just a lukewarm approach to anything, then you are not putting yourself out in the world enough to get feedback. But if you jump into something with full potential and be 'all in,' then you will immediately start getting feedback on whether you are doing things right or not. You will experience some initial quick failures and you can learn lessons from those failures.

This change in your approach towards failure will help you stay on the course in the face of failure. Because you will firmly understand, as is rightly quoted below:

> ***"Being defeated is often a temporary condition. Giving up is what makes it permanent."*** ~
> ***Marilyn vos Savant***

Final Words

> *"There are no secrets to success. It is the result of preparation, hard work and learning from failure."* – *Colin Powell*

Congratulations! You have reached the end of this book, which not many people achieve. Most people start things and leave them in between. But you are not in that category. So firstly, you should congratulate yourself for that. As we know, reading any book enhances knowledge on the subject. But our objective should be to turn that knowledge into wisdom by practical application in our lives.

If you have come so far, it simply means you are sincere about your life and your dreams. But as Napoleon Hill has said, "Knowledge is not the power. Knowledge is only a potential power. What you do with that knowledge towards your purpose and create value in the world that makes the knowledge a power."

Reading any book requires determination, effort, and an investment of time, but that gets covered under the category of consumption. Your real purpose will be served out of this book when you are able to produce the results by taking consistent action towards your goal.

Compare reading to a wrestler consuming a highly nutritional diet and building his muscles and strength, but until he produces the results in the wrestling ground, there is no real benefit in consuming that diet and building muscles.

So, I urge you to use the knowledge in this book and practically apply them in your life. It is you and only you who can take responsibility to change your life and achieve your dreams.

Therefore, tell yourself loudly these powerful lines by William Ernest Henley.

> ***"I am the master of my fate. I am the captain of my soul."***

And start taking massive action towards your goals. Success is all yours.

Cheers

Som Bathla

Thank You!

Before you go, I would like to say thank you for purchasing and reading my book.

You could have picked amongst dozens of other books on this subject, but you took a chance and checked out this one.

So, big thanks for downloading this book and reading all the way to the end.

Now I'd like to ask for a small favor. ***<u>Could you please spend a minute or two and leave a review for this book on Amazon</u>***

Reviews are really gold for authors!

Your reviews will help me continue to write the kind of books that help you get results. Also, your review will help the book to reach out to more readers.

So, just drop in 1-2 lines of your honest review on the book.

Your Free Gift Bundle:

Did you download your Gift Bundle already?

Click and Download your Free Gift Bundle Below

Claim Your Gift Bundle!

Three AMAZING BOOKS for FREE on:

1. Mind Hacking - in just 21 days!
2. Time Hacking- How to Cheat Time!
3. The Productivity Manifesto

Download Now

You can also download your gift at http://sombathla.com/freegiftbundle

Copyright © 2017 by Som Bathla

All rights reserved. No part of this book may be reproduced in any form without permission in writing from the author.

No part of this publication may be reproduced or transmitted in any form or by any means, mechanical or electronic, including photocopying or recording, or by any information storage and retrieval system, or transmitted by email or by any other means whatsoever without permission in writing from the author.

DISCLAIMER

While all attempts have been made to verify the information provided in this publication, the author does not assume any responsibility for errors, omissions, or contrary interpretations of the subject matter herein.

The views expressed are those of the author alone, and should not be taken as expert instruction or commands. The reader is responsible for his or her own actions.

The author makes no representations or warranties with respect to the accuracy or completeness of the contents of this work and specifically disclaims all warranties, including without limitation warranties of fitness for a particular purpose. No warranty may be created or extended by sales or promotional materials. The advice and recipes contained herein may not be suitable for everyone. This work is sold with the understanding that the author is not engaged in rendering medical, legal or other professional advice or services. If professional assistance is required, the services of a competent professional person should be sought. The author shall not be liable for damages arising here from. The fact that an individual, organization of website is referred to in this work as a citation and/or potential source of further information does not mean that the author endorses the information the individual, organization to website may provide or recommendations they/it may make. Further, readers should be aware that Internet websites listed in this work might have changed or disappeared between when this work was written and when it is read.

Adherence to all applicable laws and regulations, including international, federal, state, and local governing professional licensing, business practices, advertising, and all other aspects of doing business in any jurisdiction in the world is the sole responsibility of the purchaser or reader.

Printed in Great Britain
by Amazon